Vengeance
in Reverse

Vengeance in Reverse

The Tangled Loops of Violence,
Myth, and Madness

Mark R. Anspach

Michigan State University Press · *East Lansing*

♾ The paper used in this publication meets the minimum requirements
of ANSI/NISO Z39.48-1992 (R 1997) (Permanence of Paper).

Michigan State University Press
East Lansing, Michigan 48823-5245

Printed and bound in the United States of America.

26 25 24 23 22 21 20 19 18 17   1 2 3 4 5 6 7 8 9 10

LIBRARY OF CONGRESS CATALOGING-IN-PUBLICATION DATA
Names: Anspach, Mark Rogin, 1959- author.
Title: Vengeance in reverse : the tangled loops of violence, myth, and madness / Mark R. Anspach.
Description: East Lansing : Michigan State University Press, [2017] | Series: Studies in violence,
mimesis, and culture | Includes bibliographical references and index.
Identifiers: LCCN 2016027905| ISBN 9781611862386 (pbk. : alk. paper) | ISBN 9781609175207 (pdf)
| ISBN 9781628952902 (epub) | ISBN 9781628962901 (kindle)
Subjects: LCSH: Revenge—Philosophy. | Reciprocity (Psychology) | Psychoses.
Classification: LCC BF637.R48 A57 2017 | DDC 220.8/3036—dc23
LC record available at https://lccn.loc.gov/2016027905

Book design by Charlie Sharp, Sharp Des!gns, East Lansing, Michigan
Cover design by David Drummond, Salamander Design, www.salamanderhill.com
Cover image is upper part of caduceus (Hermes staff), early fifth century BCE, bronze.
Overall: 5 × 4⅛ × ¾ in. (12.7 × 10.478 × 1.905 cm). Dallas Museum of Art,
gift of the Junior League of Dallas. Used with permission.

Michigan State University Press is a member of the Green Press Initiative and is committed to developing
and encouraging ecologically responsible publishing practices. For more information about the Green
Press Initiative and the use of recycled paper in book publishing, please visit *www.greenpressinitiative.org.*

Visit Michigan State University Press at *www.msupress.org*

To the memory of my mother,
Ruth Rogin Anspach
· · ·

Contents

ix   Preface

Part 1. Changing Reciprocities

3   CHAPTER 1. Beginning with the Return, or Vengeance in Reverse

13   CHAPTER 2. Violence Deceived

27   CHAPTER 3. Trying to Stop the Trojan War

Part 2. Self-Transcendence

43   CHAPTER 4. Return to the Beginning, or the Making of a Metagod

57   CHAPTER 5. Madness in the Making

73   CHAPTER 6. No Exit? Madness and the Divided Self

101   Notes

113   Bibliography

117   Index

Preface

What is the opposite of vengeance? One answer is gift exchange or *nonviolent reciprocity*. This book takes off from the idea that peaceful exchange is like vengeance in reverse. After an opening tour through the tangled loops involved in thinking about the transition between violent and nonviolent reciprocity, we home in on peacemaking rituals to see what pre-state societies do in practice when they need to effect the tricky shift from violence to gift.

Once fighting has started, it can be devilishly hard to reverse course. Even the march toward war may take on an almost unstoppable momentum. This is what happens in a fascinating French play that reimagines the events leading up to the most famous conflict in Greek mythology. To head off the Trojan War, Hector must find a way to escape the tangled loop that can make violence a self-fulfilling prophecy.

The tale of Hector's travails brings to a close the part of the book focused on interaction between groups. The second part attacks the problem of conflict within a group. This means reframing the question with which we began: What is the opposite of vengeance?

If vengeance is defined as violent reciprocity, the answer will be the one given above: nonviolent reciprocity. But if it is defined as reciprocal violence, then the answer will be *nonreciprocal violence*. A group may overcome recip-rocal violence within its ranks by uniting against a single victim. René Girard has argued persuasively that nonreciprocal, all-against-one violence of this kind is at the very origin of social order.

A stunning series of myths from ancient India transport us back to a like moment of origin and give us a chance to witness something rarely seen with such clarity: the progressive, step-by-step *emergence of transcendence*. This return to the mist-shrouded beginning of politics and religion uncovers the tangled loop through which a unanimous group creates its own divinity.

Or rather, almost unanimous: the individual at the center is excluded. It is therefore more accurate to speak of *unanimity minus one*. What might a configuration of unanimity minus one look like from the vantage point of the "one"? According to French psychiatrist Henri Grivois, patients in the throes of a psychotic break invariably feel they have been mysteriously thrust to the center of everyone else. Collective myths and individual delusions are rooted in symmetrical processes of self-transcendence.

But individual delusion may also be approached from a different angle, that of *self*-delusion. Once we have understood the entry into madness, we must try to fathom why the journey out is so hard. With the help of Gregory Bateson and Jean-Paul Sartre, we zoom in on the paradoxical structure of consciousness: the self-transcendence of the self "itself." The overall move-ment of part 2 is thus a descending one that tracks the phenomenon of self-transcendence as it manifests itself within the collectivity, between the collectivity and the individual, and inside the individual mind.

This descending movement stops short before reaching the bedrock enigma of how the conscious mind emerges from its material or symbolic substrate. That ultimate riddle is the one that inspired Douglas Hofstadter to coin the expressions "strange loop" and "tangled hierarchy." While my allusions to "tangled loops" are meant as an homage to Hofstadter, this book tackles other conundrums. How do humans stop fighting? Where do the gods of myth come from? What does it mean to go mad?

Let me add a brief word about the division of the book into two parts. The first three chapters on back-and-forth changes in reciprocity form a cycle devoted to what might be called horizontal interaction. The follow-ing three chapters on self-transcendence take the analysis to another level by introducing a vertical dimension. In short, the transition between parts 1 and

2 itself embodies the pivotal shift out of horizontal reciprocity via the change of levels that characterizes self-transcendence.

My approach to self-transcendence is indebted to Jean-Pierre Dupuy, whose intellectual influence will be evident throughout. Most of the book is rooted in work I did in the stimulating environment of two institutes he cofounded, the Centre de Recherche en Épistémologie Appliquée in Paris and the Program of Interdisciplinary Research at Stanford.

My current work is conducted under the auspices of Imitatio, a project of the Thiel Foundation. I am grateful to Peter Thiel, Lindy Fishburne, Jimmy Kaltreider, and the late Robert Hamerton-Kelly for their support. Special thanks go to Bill Johnsen for prodding me to bring out a book in English and for welcoming it in the distinguished series he edits.

In shaping the manuscript into its final form, I profited greatly from exchanges with Trevor Merrill. He and my brother, William Anspach, helped me find the right title for the book.

I would like to express my appreciation to Doctor Henri Grivois, whose theory of madness I discuss in chapter 5, for giving me the chance to observe his work with patients in the psychiatric clinic he directed at a public hospital in the center of Paris. Doctor Grivois also drew my attention to the curious statement by Esquirol's patient that became the point of departure for the reflections in chapter 6. William Anspach put me on the right track for that chapter's treatment of Sartre.

My understanding of violence and myth is grounded in the mimetic theory of René Girard, whose writings I first discovered as an undergraduate at Harvard. He offered me valuable early encouragement and helped determine the subsequent course of my career by introducing me to Jean-Pierre Dupuy at the 1981 Stanford symposium on "Disorder and Order" just as I was preparing to leave for graduate study in Europe. Later, when I came back to Stanford for a PhD, I had the privilege of serving as René's research assistant. I will always be grateful for the time I was fortunate enough to spend with him over the years and will miss him as will all those whose lives he touched.

●   ■   ■

The texts that make up this book originated as separate articles, but I have revised all of them to a greater or lesser extent for the purposes of the present volume. In particular, I have expanded considerably the exposition in chapter 4 and updated chapters 1 and 6 with new material.

"Beginning with the Return, or Vengeance in Reverse" was originally published as "Vengeance in Reverse: Reconciliation through Exchange" in *Stanford French Review* 16, no. 1 (1992): 77–85. "Violence Deceived" was originally published as "Violence Deceived: Changing Reciprocities from Vengeance to Gift Exchange" in *Expanding the Economic Concept of Exchange: Deception, Self-Deception and Illusions*, ed. Caroline Gerschlager (Boston: Kluwer, 2001), 213–24. "Trying to Stop the Trojan War" was originally published as "Trying to Stop the Trojan War: Prophesying Violence, Seeing Peace" in *Western Humanities Review* 62, no. 3 (2008): 86–97.

"Return to the Beginning, or the Making of a Metagod" was originally published as "The Making of a Meta-God: Sacrifice and Self-Transcendence in Vedic Mythology" in *Paragrana: Internationale Zeitschrift für Historische Anthropologie* 4, no. 2 (1995): 117–25. "Madness in the Making" was originally published as "The Solitary Madman and the Madding Crowd: Symmetrical Morphogeneses of the Social Bond" in *Synthesis: An Interdisciplinary Journal* 1, no. 1 (1995): 129–45.

"No Exit? Madness and the Divided Self" was originally published as "Madness and the Divided Self: Esquirol, Sartre, Bateson" in *Self-Deception and Paradoxes of Rationality*, ed. Jean-Pierre Dupuy (Stanford: CSLI Publications, 1998), 59–85. Reprinted, with permission, from CSLI Publications. Copyright 1998 by CSLI Publications, Stanford University, Stanford, CA 94305.

PART 1

Changing Reciprocities

CHAPTER 1

Beginning with the Return, or Vengeance in Reverse

Even when the avenger kills his victim he is doing no more than obeying a clause of unwritten law. And so these time-honored and unspoken rules go on twisting themselves around these people's legs throughout their lives, until the day comes when they inevitably trip them up.

— Ismail Kadare, *The General of the Dead Army*

I would like to start out by reflecting a little on what it means to think of vengeance as an exchange of violence. And the first thing I would like to do is to suggest that vengeance is *not* an exchange of violence.

What is exchange? An exchange takes place when something is passed back and forth between people, or when something is passed in one direction and something else in the other. And I say advisedly: some *thing*. There is some thing moving between the exchange partners. There is an object. Now, it is obvious that the expression "exchange of violence" can only be metaphorical from this point of view. There may be an exchange of blows, but there is no object transferred back and forth.

The metaphor of an exchange of violence is seductive because it is easy to see a resemblance or parallel between an exchange of blows or an exchange of hostilities and other forms of exchange. Not only is there a parallel in structure, there often seems to be a real continuity, as Claude Lévi-Strauss asserts in a frequently cited passage of *The Elementary Structures of Kinship*: "There is a link, a continuity, between hostile relations and the provision of reciprocal prestations. Exchanges are peacefully resolved wars, and wars are the result of unsuccessful transactions."[1] A French anthropologist, Alfred Adler, has commented on this passage as follows:

> That there is an oscillation between peaceful exchange and war, that groups periodically face the choice of either dealing with the other or of taking by force at the risk of losing everything—the facts are there that bear witness to this. The error is to suppose that the terms of the choice are in a relation of analogy and that this analogy can serve as an explanation, by privileging either one term (everything is exchange and war is an exchange gone wrong) or the other (everything is war and peaceful exchange is but a modality of it).[2]

My premise is that neither war nor exchange is primary, but rather reciprocity. The latter is ambivalent—alternately good or bad.[3] I want to distinguish the abstract *form* of reciprocity from the phenomenon of exchange. Exchange is one type of reciprocity, violent reciprocity another. The difference is that in exchange there is an object that acts as a mediator. Anthropologists and sociologists often look at exchange as a kind of web that weaves society together. But while exchange does draw people together, it also separates them, at least in the minimal sense that it places an object between them.

Such a minimal separation may hardly seem worth mentioning. The best way to realize its importance is to see what happens when it does not exist. In fact, a dispute between two people turns violent at the precise moment that a literal absence of separation occurs—for example, an absence of separation between one person's nose and the other person's fist. At that moment there is nothing left *between* the antagonists. An object may have *come between* them in the sense that it was an object of contention. But, and this is something that René Girard has described well, once a conflict escalates to the point of violence, the antagonists tend to lose sight of the ostensible object of contention. The violence takes on its own momentum, and the original object drops from view. No thing is exchanged. All that remains is the pure form of reciprocity. That is why in the case of violence I prefer to speak of reciprocity rather than exchange.

One may place the various types of reciprocity along a continuum running from the pure reciprocity of violence to the peaceful exchange of gifts. To employ a common terminology, reciprocity is negative at one pole and positive at the other. In fact, the move from negative to positive reciprocity means something more than just a change from bad to good, from the infelicitous act of fighting to the happier gesture of giving. The terms "negative" and "positive" are even more apt than they might seem. An actual reversal in orientation occurs between the two poles. But before homing in on the shift from the vendetta to gift exchange, we need to recognize that a transition must first be made between the pure reciprocity of violence and the vendetta taken as an empirical ethnographic phenomenon.

The extreme form of immediate, unalloyed reciprocity is what society must avoid at all cost. No community can long tolerate an outbreak of spontaneous, uncontrolled violence. Yet the anthropologist Raymond Verdier holds that while there is always a danger of vengeance rampaging out of control, real-world vengeance in the cultures that practice it often proves to be a smoothly functioning system, which he has dubbed the "vindicatory system."[4] Here he makes a distinction between the *vindicatif* and the *vindicatoire*, the spontaneous vindictive impulse that prompts an individual to lash back, and the vindicatory system as a social institution with rules and regulations enshrined in tradition. From this point of view, Verdier maintains, vengeance is not at all the dangerously uncontrolled phenomenon that René Girard's discussion of it in *Violence and the Sacred* could lead one to believe.

"There is the risk that the act of vengeance will initiate a chain reaction whose consequences will quickly prove fatal to any society of modest size," writes Girard. "The multiplication of reprisals instantaneously puts the very existence of a society in jeopardy, and that is why it is universally proscribed."[5] Verdier would no doubt retort that in many cultures revenge is a sacred duty incumbent on a member of the tribe, a social imperative for the man of honor—in short, an obligation. Far from *pro*scribing vengeance, the society *pre*scribes it.

Lucien Scubla has shown how socially prescribed vengeance follows ritual forms that are part of a larger sacrificial system, so that the vindicatory system can be said to control vengeance by virtue of the fact that it is itself sacrificial.[6] I would like to make another point by drawing attention to the basic paradox at issue here. We have a phenomenon that in its spontaneous form must be avoided, and instead of proscribing it, it is prescribed. What kind of crazy prescription is that? An analogy can be found in the psycho-therapeutic technique known as "prescribing the symptom." This technique is used precisely when the symptom to be cured is a self-destructive spontane-ous behavior that the patient cannot control. The psychologists of the Palo Alto school explain that prescribing the symptom works because it creates a therapeutic double bind.

Gregory Bateson employed the expression "double bind" to describe paradoxical imperatives with which one cannot comply without falling headlong into noncompliance. The classic case of the double bind consists in commanding someone to do something that can only be spontaneous, such as manifesting true love—"Love me for myself and not because I ask you"—or showing independence: "Don't be so submissive—stop doing everything I tell you." The very fact of demanding spontaneity creates a situation in which spontaneous behavior is impossible. That is a bad thing when the behavior in question is desirable. But the Palo Alto psychologists reason that it can be a good thing if one is treating a spontaneous behavior that is undesirable or pathological. A therapeutic double bind puts the patient "into an untenable situation with regard to his pathology. If he complies, he no longer 'can't help it'; he does 'it,' and this . . . makes 'it' impossible, which is the purpose of therapy. If he resists the injunction, he can do so only by *not* behaving symptomatically, which is the purpose of therapy."[7]

Let me give an example that does not involve vengeance, but conflict within a family. Watzlawick, Beavin, and Jackson describe a family in therapy where one daughter in particular continually argues with everyone else and does everything she can to sidetrack discussion. Finally, she announces that she will no longer cooperate with the therapy at all. The therapist's response is to tell her that this is a good thing because he wants her to be as uncoopera-tive as possible. This puts her in a double bind because if she continues to be disruptive, she is cooperating with the therapy, while her only alternative is to stop being disruptive and uncooperative.[8]

It would be a mistake to push the analogy too far. I am obviously not sug-gesting that there is some great therapist in the sky guiding human culture.

Still, the example is interesting inasmuch as it demonstrates that commanding conflict may suffice to get a measure of cooperation going. That accords well with Raymond Verdier's observation that a vindicatory system functions as a kind of "game with rules" where rival groups vie for superiority without trying to destroy each other.[9] Such a game entails not only an effort to outdo the other party but also an unspoken agreement to keep the rivalry within mutually acceptable bounds. This notion of a game with rules is not so far from Girard's idea that enemy tribes may operate under an "agreement for the sake of hostility," making a tacit deal to cooperate in providing each other with victims through continuing, ritualized reciprocal violence.[10]

Let me give one more example of prescribing the symptom that is likewise suggestive in the context of vengeance. If a patient complains of chronic pain with no physiological basis and the therapist is sure the pain is psychogenic, the therapist may tell the patient that it is not possible to eliminate the pain, but that the patient should be able to "shift the pain in time" and to "telescope its intensity." For example, the patient may be told to pick a two-hour period of the day in which it would be least inconvenient to feel more pain, and to increase the pain during those two hours. "The extraordinary thing about this," the Palo Alto psychologists observe, "is that patients usually manage to feel worse at the time selected, as suggested, and by going through this experience they cannot fail to realize that somehow they have control over their pain."[11] I have been arguing that rendering vengeance nonspontaneous makes it susceptible to control. One of the ways this control manifests itself is precisely by circumscribing the phenomenon in time and space. I propose to call this the "telescoping" of vengeance.

Here we may take as an example the highly codified practice of revenge in the northern Albanian highlands, which Ismail Kadare describes memorably in a novel cited by Verdier, *Broken April*.[12] The Albanian vendetta telescopes the most intense vengeance into the hours immediately following the murder, when members of the victim's family, blinded by the blood that has just been spilled, have the right to avenge themselves on any member of the killer's family. However, the killer's family has the right to ask the victim's family for a truce of twenty-four hours, which is usually granted, provided that the killer has comported himself in accordance with custom. This initial truce is usually followed by a longer truce of thirty days, giving the killer time to seek shelter in one of the refuge towers that dot the landscape. These towers are considered inviolable sanctuaries. Once inside their walls, a killer cannot be touched. In short, after telescoping the passionate vindictive impulse into a very brief interval, the rules impose a number of limits in time and space by which vengeance is strictly controlled. As a result, Albania's centuries-old vindicatory system has not proved fatal to the society.

Yet it is hardly without drawbacks. If too many men are embroiled in feuds and lock themselves up in refuge towers, the fields will go untended. Often, according to Kadare, a quarter of the fields in a given area would lie fallow for that reason—sometimes a third or even half—and food would run short.[13] Such is the price of leaving the regulation of violence to a vindicatory system. It is no wonder that Albania's twentieth-century rulers sought to change things. This was no easy task, as a modernizing monarch learned in the interwar years. "While campaigning against hereditary blood feuds," recalls Balkans expert Elizabeth Pond, "the suspicious King Zog also killed so many putative rivals that he greatly increased the number of vendettas; he alone was personally involved in an estimated 600 feuds and survived some fifty-five assassination attempts."[14]

After World War II, the Stalinist dictator Enver Hoxha, though no less intolerant of rivals, proved more successful at establishing a state monopoly on violent retribution. At the time Kadare wrote *Broken April*, the practices depicted in the novel had been ruthlessly suppressed and were largely a thing of the past. Those who dared violate the ban on taking revenge were sometimes buried alive in the coffins of their victims.[15] However grotesque, this method of punishment was doubtless not as arbitrary as it sounds. In a ritual context where blood must be paid with blood, burying a killer alive would have been a way to take his life without spilling new blood—an expedient designed to cut short the cycle of reprisals and bury the feud along with the feuders.

Unfortunately, with the loosening of the state's iron grip on society after the fall of communism, the blood feud returned with a vengeance. By 1996, some sixty thousand people were estimated to be caught up in feuds.[16] Thousands died before the phenomenon could be brought under control. Although the number of victims has declined in recent years, the blood feud remains, in the words of a University of Tirana researcher, "a serious social plague."[17] Any of a killer's male relatives become fair game as soon as they venture outside their house. In one case cited by an American reporter, "a dozen men had been forced indoors after a male family member killed a shopkeeper who refused to sell his child an ice cream cone."[18] Another feud that claimed half a dozen lives began when a man shot a drinking companion for tactlessly reminding him that his family had backed down in a previous feud half a century before. Asked what that earlier feud was about, the man's sister-in-law could only shake her head. "It all happened so long ago," she said.[19]

A vendetta can easily last for generations, long after anyone remembers what original offense started it. The problem is that, in a sense, no one ever starts such a conflict—it always seems to be the other side that is responsible for provoking you, while your retaliation is liable to appear unwarranted or excessive to them. Alfred Adler speaks in this regard of a lack of "common measure": "The legitimate murder perpetrated by the avenger or avengers runs the risk of bringing on counter-reprisals, insofar as the adverse party may deem the loss it has suffered to be disproportionate."[20] There is in general what Jean-Pierre Dupuy, borrowing another expression from Gregory Bateson, calls a problem of "punctuation," with each side identifying differently which terms in the sequence of reprisals are offensive provocations and which constitute just retribution.[21] Since the parties cannot agree on the beginning, they have trouble agreeing on the end. New individuals are perpetually drawn in as avengers and victims-to-be for the simple reason that the murder victim is not usually able to avenge himself. I say "usually" because an exception does exist that I will describe at the end of this chapter.

How, then, is it possible to escape this endless chain of negative reciprocity? Here is where we encounter the reversal in orientation of which I spoke earlier. So far, I have argued that the way out of *spontaneous* violent reciprocity is to *prescribe* violent reciprocity. I now want to suggest that the way out of *non*spontaneous violent reciprocity is to prescribe reciprocity pure and simple. The great French Sanskrit scholar Charles Malamoud once remarked to me that the difference between vengeance and gift exchange is that in vengeance one does not seek reciprocity. One does not do something to someone else so that they will do something to you. The return is not wanted like a return gift, yet each action does provoke a return, so that everyone hurtles endlessly onward in the wrong direction. The way to overcome this process is once again to foresee it and to prescribe it, which I submit means to seize the initiative by beginning with the return. In gift exchange, there is a sense in which the initial gift is already the return gift. If you receive a gift from someone to whom you have given a gift, it is, quite simply, because that person has already received their return gift from you.

Compared to the negative reciprocity of vengeance, the positive reciprocity of the gift involves a reversal in temporal orientation. In negative reciprocity, you take action against someone else, and then they make you pay the price by taking action against you. In positive reciprocity, on the other hand, you pay the price first: you begin by taking action against yourself, in the sense that you give up something, and then they take action against themselves—they give up something. They give up something after having already gotten their revenge on you. Of course, one might object that giving a gift should be a pleasure, not a self-destructive act. I am really thinking here of ritualized gift-giving in pre-state societies where the gift is identified with the giver and where I would contend that it is sacrificed by the giver in a kind of limited self-sacrifice—one sacrifices the gift in one's own stead.[22] As Marcel Mauss writes in his classic work *The Gift*, "by giving one is giving *oneself*."[23]

Notice that the transition from violent reciprocity to gift exchange does not entail substituting the gift for violence as one exchange object for another. As I argued at the outset, there is no exchange in the pure reciprocity of violence. The violence stops when an object is interposed between the partners; the exchange object is a substitute, not for the violence, but for the giver. It is the use of a substitute to deflect violence that can properly be called sacrificial in René Girard's sense of the term.

I am going to close this chapter with two examples that prefigure the temporal inversion by which vengeance may be transformed into its opposite. First, I would like to return to the novel *Broken April*. The title refers to the end of the protagonist's thirty-day truce. The novel begins on March 17, when Gjorg kills his brother's killer. We are told that he feels time will stop for him on April 17, when his truce will end and, whether or not he dies immediately, he will effectively leave the world of the living. The novel ends on April 17, when Gjorg is in fact killed the moment his truce expires. Now, a funny thing happens at that moment. Not only does time stop, it shifts into reverse.

Here I will quote from the last paragraph of Kadare's novel. While Gjorg lies dying on the ground, the retreating footsteps of his murderer echo in his ears:

Again, he heard footsteps, drawing away, and a number of times he wondered, whose steps are those? He felt that they were familiar. Yes, he knew them... They're mine! The seventeenth of March, the road, near Brezftoht ... He lost consciousness for a moment, then he heard the footsteps again, and again it seemed to him that they were his own, that it was himself and no one else who was running now, leaving behind, sprawled on the road, his own body that he had just struck down.[24]

Gjorg recognizes the murderer's footsteps as his own, and suddenly it is no longer April 17; he is back on March 17, except that this time his victim is himself. In fact, he knew on March 17 that by entering into the chain of vengeance he was signing his own death warrant—he might as well have been killing himself.[25]

So why not imagine a system of vengeance in reverse, where one kills oneself and then one's adversary kills himself? That is indeed the example with which I will end. It is exactly what we find in eighteenth-century Japan where, and this is the exceptional case I mentioned earlier, tradition made it possible for a murder victim to avenge himself—provided that he was his own murder victim. A nobleman who was grievously offended by another nobleman had the option of demonstrating the depth of his outrage by committing seppuku. If he did so, he died secure in the knowledge that, to avoid losing face, the offending party would likewise be obliged to commit suicide.[26]

This custom substitutes reciprocal self-sacrifice for reciprocal murder. By killing himself first, the Japanese nobleman reverses the ordinary logic of vengeance. But the most common form of vengeance in reverse is the reciprocal self-sacrifice of gift exchange. Once one has caught on to the trick of turning negative reciprocity around, it is generally preferable to sacrifice an object instead of oneself. By shifting from war to the rivalry in gift-giving that marks the potlatch, people learned, in the words of Mauss, how "to oppose one another without massacring one another and to give themselves without sacrificing themselves."[27] Or, as I would put it: how to sacrifice themselves without carnage, cheating violence of its victory. It is time now to examine more closely just how violence is deceived.

CHAPTER 2

Violence Deceived

aroline Gerschlager has drawn attention to the close affinity between the German words for exchange and deception: *tauschen* and *täuschen*.[1] An old German saying plays on the similarity between the two terms: "He who has the desire to exchange has the desire to deceive."[2] Is there some sense in which we may regard deception as "a *constituent quality of exchange*"?[3]

All sorts of dirty tricks can be employed to get the better of an exchange partner. No matter how underhanded such tactics may be, they still fall short of foul play pure and simple. Trickery, like hypocrisy, is a tribute that vice pays to virtue. It is defined not only by a willingness to stretch the rules of peaceful exchange, but by an unwillingness to break them outright. Using cunning to obtain what one wants means refraining from using brute force. There is an important difference between sharp dealing and a blow with a blunt instrument.

Now, nothing is easier than coming to blows, and nothing is more dangerous, particularly in pre-state societies with no judicial authorities and no police to keep violence from spreading. That is why one could argue that the earliest and most vital function of economic exchange is not economic at all. Trading goods keeps people from trading blows—and that's a pretty neat trick right there. It is, in fact, the trick we will study in this chapter: not deception within exchange transactions, but the kind of deception necessary to get peaceful exchange started in the first place. This deception takes place at a metalevel. It is a ruse making it possible to effect a metaexchange between two types of exchange—to exchange negative for positive reciprocity, the exchange of blows for the exchange of gifts.

Going to Extremes

The empirical proximity and apparent structural equivalence between violent and nonviolent reciprocity are a recurring theme in French anthropological theory. In the previous chapter, I quoted Lévi-Strauss's assertion that "a link, a continuity" exists between hostile relations and reciprocal prestations: "Exchanges are peacefully resolved wars, and wars are the result of unsuccessful transactions."[4] This symmetrical formulation seems to place peaceful and hostile exchanges on the same footing. Superficially at least, they are presented as interchangeable, almost as if one could go back and forth between them at will.

A similar treatment of the relationship between violence and peaceful exchange is found in Lévi-Strauss's illustrious predecessor Marcel Mauss. At the end of his essay *The Gift*, Mauss sums things up by saying that if men "have been able to commit themselves to giving and giving in return," that is because there was "no choice," for when two groups meet, they "can only either draw apart, and, if they show mistrust towards one another or issue a challenge, fight"—or else they can come to terms. So it is that men have "approached one another in a curious frame of mind, one of fear and exaggerated hostility, and of generosity that was likewise exaggerated." When generosity prevails over hostility, "one gives everything, from fleeting acts of hospitality to one's daughter and one's goods." But whichever way one goes, one must go all the way: "one trusts completely, or one mistrusts completely." Indeed, Mauss emphasizes, "there is no middle way."[5]

This seems to be a case of the "excluded middle." *Il n'y a pas de milieu*:[6] no middle ground exists between the extremes of reciprocal hostility or reciprocal generosity; it is either one or the other. At the same time, however, Mauss also suggests that it is easy to shift back and forth between these two extremes. He speaks of an "instability" between war and the kind of festivals where gifts are exchanged. And here we may wonder how it is possible for two types of relation to be at once diametrically opposed and interchangeable. If there is no middle term, how does one move from one to the other? How, in Lévi-Strauss's language, is the "link" or "continuity" achieved?

We will return to these questions later. What I would like to do now is take a close look at the two examples Mauss uses to illustrate the sudden shifts that can take place. The first example is of a change in a positive direction, from hostility to generosity:

> In the Trobriand Islands the people of Kiriwina told Malinowski: "The men from Dobu are not good like us; they are cruel, they are cannibals. When we come to Dobu, we are afraid of them. They might kill us. But then I spit out ginger root, and their attitude changes. They lay down their spears and receive us well."[7]

It is here that Mauss uses the term "instability": "Nothing better conveys this instability between festival and war."[8]

Mauss then proceeds to give an example of a change in a negative direction, from generosity to hostility. This second example, involving another Melanesian tribe, "also clearly demonstrates how these people, as a group, suddenly pass from festival to battle":

> Buleau, a chief, had invited another chief, Bobal, and his people to a banquet, probably the first in a long series. They began to rehearse the dances the whole night through. In the morning they were all in a state of nerves from their sleepless night, the dances, and the songs. As a result of a simple remark made by Buleau, one of Bobal's men killed him. And the rank and file massacred, pillaged, and carried off the women of the village.

Mauss concludes his account of this incident with a terse comment that may make us wonder what kind of company he kept: "We have all observed such facts, even around us."[9]

Although most of us have probably never witnessed such extreme behavior—not even when those around us are in a state of nerves—we do know how suddenly the most elaborately organized festivities can go awry if one guest takes umbrage at a remark made by another, and how abruptly a cordial relationship can be cut short by a perceived insult or unintended slight. We can therefore understand the kind of instability Mauss is talking about. What I want to suggest is that this instability is largely one-way. An accidental occurrence can provoke durable hostilities, but a successful gathering or a long-term friendly relationship do not generally come about by accident—they require a concerted effort. And the most difficult thing of all is to produce friendly exchanges between people who are fighting. Gift exchange doesn't just break out spontaneously between antagonists in the same way that conflict can break out between exchange partners.

A careful examination of Mauss's two examples will reveal that they do not disprove the one-way character of the instability in question. While the first example depicts a change in a peaceful direction, it is not truly symmetrical with the second example demonstrating how these people "suddenly pass from festival to battle." We are not shown anyone passing with equal suddenness from battle to festival. The first example does not involve individuals who actually stopped fighting, but only ones who might potentially have fought, yet did not. What is missing is a concrete example of how those who have already begun fighting manage to stop. Mauss merely observes in general terms that it "is by opposing reason to feeling, by pitting the will to peace against sudden outbursts of insanity of this kind that peoples succeed in substituting alliance, gifts, and trade for war, isolation, and stagnation."[10] This is no doubt true enough, yet it hardly seems adequate to invoke reason and the will to peace. We still need to know *how* gifts and trade are substituted for violence. If, as Lévi-Strauss puts it, exchanges are peacefully resolved wars, how are the wars resolved so that the exchanges may take place?

Looking Forward or Striking Back

Lévi-Strauss's formulation displays a comparable asymmetry. It is not clear how the shift to peaceful exchange is accomplished, since the war must be successfully resolved first. On the other hand, it is clear enough how war can be the result of *un*successful transactions—all it takes is for the peaceful exchange to fail. Indeed, the failure to return a gift may in some circumstances provoke hostilities. The giver may expect a return, but the receiver might not cooperate by making one, and the giver will be disappointed. To be sure, the giver may not want the return gift to match his initial gift—he may hope his own generosity will outshine the other's—but, even in the case of such competitive giving, he is apt to be insulted if the other makes no attempt at all to reciprocate. The giver does want the receiver to recognize his positive gesture; he looks forward to the return. In this sense, gift-giving involves an orientation toward the future. But there is always the risk that the future gift will never come, that positive reciprocity will break down, and perhaps even give way to negative reciprocity.

Once negative reciprocity has emerged, however, it will tend to continue indefinitely into the future precisely because the same kind of future orientation is lacking. For example, someone may insult someone else on the spur of the moment, without any thought for the consequences. The other may react to what has happened by killing him. He will do so as reparation for the past offense and not because he looks forward to being killed in turn. Yet the victim's son or brother or cousin is liable to avenge the victim out of a need to strike back or even things out. The avenger does not look forward to being killed either, yet the new victim's relatives may feel things are not truly even until they have gotten even in turn. In the same way, each new murder may call for reprisal, without an equilibrium's ever being reached, so that the vendetta continues of its own momentum. In this sense, negative reciprocity feeds on its own failure: the failure to settle accounts once and for all.

That is why the instability between positive and negative reciprocity tends to be one-way: whereas the failure of a peaceful transaction may trigger a spontaneous shift into vengeance, vengeance will continue spontaneously out of its failure to reverse the past. The avengers seek to wipe out a past event and end up provoking its repetition. The key is the difference in temporal orientation between an exchange of gifts and an exchange of blows. A murderer is not looking for a return blow, but the return comes looking for him. It is because the partners in a vendetta are not forward-looking that the vendetta goes forward of its own accord.

Reciprocal violence perpetuates itself almost like an autonomous force, a force more powerful than the individuals who find themselves swept up in it. Whereas peaceful exchange depends on human intentions, violent reciprocity tends to transcend human will. The problem, then, is how to tame this potentially overpowering force and bring it under human control. The answer, I believe, is that if this superhuman force cannot be denied, it can be deceived. A custom described by the anthropologist Robert Lowie will show how the deception can be accomplished.

In *Primitive Society*, Lowie contrasts the way two different communities, the Chukchi and the Ifugao, deal with murder and blood revenge: "The Chukchi generally make peace after the first act of retribution," Lowie says, "but among the Ifugao the struggle may go on almost interminably."[11] So what's the Chukchi's secret? Is there a trick to cutting the violence short after a single reprisal? Indeed there is, and Lowie soon reveals it: "While the Ifugao tend to protect a kinsman under almost all circumstances, the Chukchi often avert a feud by killing a member of the family."[12] In other words, after killing a member of the enemy group, they kill one of their own—not the original killer himself, but another member of the family.[13]

How does this trick succeed in breaking the cycle of vengeance? It works by looking to the future and anticipating the violence to come. Once the violence has been anticipated, it can be deceived by being diverted onto a target other than the original killer himself—a neutral target, an innocent victim. To keep the other group from striking back, the original killer's fellows anticipate the return blow and let it fall on another member of their own group. By carrying out this follow-up act of violence themselves, they dispense the adversary group from having to do so, and there is therefore no need for the violent reciprocity to continue.

The key here is the anticipation of the return. Rather than waiting for the enemy to strike back, the Chukchi offer up a victim in advance, as if they were making a gift to the other side. Indeed, I would argue that the trick used in these circumstances by the Chukchi is the same trick that underlies positive gift exchange. In positive reciprocity, the return is not only anticipated, it is, in effect, given in advance. When you receive a gift from someone to whom you have given a gift, it is as if that person had already received your return gift before the fact. You had already offered up, if not yourself or a member of your family, at the very least an object that serves as an extension of yourself. Mauss emphasizes that there is always an identification between the gift and the giver. Moreover, in the case of the potlatch, the object offered up may actually be destroyed, so that it functions as a veritable substitute victim.[14]

As I suggested before, positive reciprocity is really negative reciprocity in reverse. Changing reciprocities involves changing the temporal orientation of the reciprocity. But this is presumably easier said than done. We still have not seen exactly how the switch from vengeance to gift is accomplished in practice, although the Chukchi custom has put us on the right track.

Sacrifice and (Self-)Deception

I have borrowed the foregoing example from the opening chapter of René Girard's pioneering work *Violence and the Sacred* while taking the interpretation in a somewhat different direction. My emphasis up to now has been on the anticipation of the return, which I see as prefiguring the logic of the gift. For his part, Girard stresses the displacement of the violence onto an arbitrary victim, which he sees as laying bare the logic of sacrifice. The Chukchi custom resembles a sacrifice insofar as the victim is not the person guilty of the first murder. By excluding the guilty party himself from retribution, Girard suggests, the Chukchi seek to break out of the endlessly repetitive chain reaction of vengeance.[15]

Freedom from the risk of vengeance constitutes the defining feature of sacrifice for Girard. It is the isolated and controlled character of sacrificial violence that distinguishes it from other forms of violence. The same indiscriminate quality that can cause violence to spread out of control is also what renders it amenable to manipulation. Like the ogres or dragons of fairy tales who are given a stone to swallow in the place of the child they covet, violence can be tricked into spending its fury on a relatively indifferent victim. This victim is effectively a substitute for all the members of the community who take part in the ritual and who would themselves be at risk were reciprocal violence not contained.[16] The participation of the whole community in the sacrifice is also a way of containing the violence: since everybody shares responsibility for the victim's death, there is nobody left to avenge the killing.

From the community's point of view, ultimate responsibility for the victim's death lies with the divinity who demands sacrificial offerings from the faithful. Just as the sacrificial victim substitutes for the members of the community in their capacity as potential victims of violence, the sacrificial god substitutes for them in their capacity as potential agents of violence.[17] Insofar as the god does not exist, the deception of violence through sacrifice also involves *self*-deception on the part of the believers. If sacrifice is a ruse used to outwit human violence, it is a ruse of which the perpetrators are themselves the dupes. The god hungry for blood-offerings is a mask obscuring the all-too-human face of the violence festering in the community's midst. At the same time, since the human violence behind the divine mask is perfectly real, the sacrificial cult is based on more than a mere flight of fancy. Indeed, inasmuch as reciprocal violence genuinely threatens to overpower the individuals who find themselves in its grip, even the notion that it constitutes a transcendent force is not without a real basis. Projecting this transcendent force outside the community in the imaginary form of a sacrificial god operates as a real means of bringing it to bay. The ruse works.

Occupying a middle ground between the two extremes of exaggerated generosity toward sacrifice and equally exaggerated hostility, Girard's theory neither accepts sacrificial religions at face value nor rejects them out of hand as lacking any basis in fact. To take them at face value would mean falling into irrationality. But to dismiss them as purely irrational would make it hard to account for the role they have played throughout human history. Viewing them as the instruments of a useful ruse allows us to grasp the reason behind such extravagant displays of unreason. The ruse works, as we have just seen, through a process of substitution—that is, by exchanging one thing for another. But that is not all. By also substituting one temporal orientation for another, sacrifice makes it possible to effect an exchange between two types of exchange.

Changing Reciprocities

In my view, then, sacrifice is at once a way out of the negative reciprocity of vengeance, as Girard contends, and a way into the positive reciprocity of gift exchange, to which Girard has devoted comparatively little attention. Indeed, this dual aspect of sacrifice helps account for the widely divergent interpretations to which it has given rise. Many anthropological theorists have downplayed the destructive side of sacrifice, defining it along the lines first laid down in the late nineteenth century by Edward B. Tylor and

Robertson Smith, respectively, as an offering to a divinity and an occasion for the communal sharing of food among humans. Depending on which side of the ritual is highlighted, it can thus appear as either a destructive act of violence or a peaceful gift offering. In reality, not only is sacrifice usually both of these at once, but, I would argue, it derives its pivotal importance precisely from its capacity to embody these two aspects simultaneously.

The articulation between the two is best seen by looking at how sacrifice is used in peace ceremonies. This is a type of sacrifice that Girard, curiously, does not consider. Indeed, Girard maintains that the Chukchi ritual cannot be deemed sacrificial because a true sacrifice is never directly and openly linked to an irregular act of bloodshed.[18] This is not quite accurate. While many or most ritual sacrifices are not tied to nonsacrificial bloodshed, when it is necessary to put an end to a blood feud, the reconciliation ceremony generally does involve the performance of a sacrifice.[19] And the sacrifice is typically followed by a sharing-out of the meat among the participants that, in turn, inaugurates a series of peaceful gift exchanges. In this manner, the same rite that closes a cycle of negative reciprocity also opens a cycle of positive reciprocity.

Now we are able to answer the question as to how the shift between violence and gift is accomplished. Occupying an intermediate position, sacrifice is the missing middle term excluded from Mauss's formulations quoted earlier. It cannot be defined as exemplifying either hostility or generosity because it embodies both at once. The gap between the two is bridged when the victim of the sacrificial violence becomes the first peaceful gift offering.

As the last act of hostility, the sacrifice redirects the violence against a neutral victim, breaking the cycle of vengeance. As the first act of generosity, it redirects the reciprocity in a positive direction, launching a cycle of nonviolent exchange. Sacrifice thus owes its pivotal position to its unique combination of nonreciprocity in violence and nonviolence in reciprocity. It brings violent reciprocity to an end by separating the violence from the reciprocity, diverting the violence toward the victim and allowing the reciprocity to resume in nonviolent fashion.

The reciprocity resumes only after pausing to reverse course, however. If there is indeed a link between war and peaceful exchange, as Lévi-Strauss asserts, there is not a direct continuity. After all, one seldom sees the same party receive a blow and give a gift in return. For a vendetta to be peacefully resolved, there must be an interruption in the reciprocity followed by a change in direction. This means that the party that gave the last blow must also give the first gift.

A Daribi peace ceremony from highland New Guinea, described by Pierre Lemonnier in his book *Guerres et festins*, provides a dramatic illustration of how the shift from war to festival is achieved through the intermediary of sacrifice. In New Guinea, pork is the most appreciated dish at festive occasions. To make peace after a murder, the killer's group must bring pigs to the victim's group. As the emissaries approach leading their pigs, the intended recipients raise their bows to take aim at the men before slowly lowering their weapons to kill the animals.[20]

It is at the precise moment that the arrow is lowered that the reversal in the direction of the reciprocity takes place. If the arrow were to strike the man, the victim's group would "pay back" the killer's group for the blow received; when it strikes the pig, the killer's group "pays off" the victim's group for the blow given. To lower the weapon is to change reciprocities.

"To trade," Mauss writes, "the first condition was to be able to lay down the spear."[21] And to lay down the spear, reason and the will to peace were undoubtedly necessary. But were they enough? If the skewered pig is any guide, an exchange between two types of victim preceded the exchange between two types of exchange. Violence had to be deceived with a substitute victim before gifts and trade could be made to substitute for war.

From Hunting Animals to Offering Them

Of course, Mauss is thinking here of a long-term historic shift toward social systems based on positive reciprocity, whereas the reconciliation ceremony substituting a pig for a human victim belongs to a context of back-and-forth alternation between negative and positive reciprocity within the same social system. If we leave the highlands of New Guinea for the forests of Siberia, however, we will find a remarkable case study of a historic shift between two different social systems based on two different types of reciprocity.[22] As analyzed by Roberte Hamayon, the shift between hunting and stock-breeding societies in Siberia offers us the opportunity to take another look at the relationship between sacrifice and changing reciprocities.

The hunter's worldview is marked by the ideological primacy of taking. In their "life-exchange" with game animals, the hunter's rule is to take first and let the animal spirits take back what they can afterward. Fear of vengeance keeps the hunters from making any explicit reference to "killing" animals. Yet this fear reveals the underlying logic of the system. Despite all the hunters' precautions, they fully expect the animals to strike back sooner or later. Indeed, when humans sicken and die, their lives are believed to have been claimed by animal spirits as compensation for the animals consumed by humans.[23] From a structural point of view, therefore, it is clear that the type of reciprocity governing relations between humans and animals is the negative reciprocity of vengeance.

With the disappearance of hunting and the adoption of stock-breeding, however, a dramatic change occurs in "the whole system of relationships with the natural environment": "the impulse shifts from 'taking' to 'giving.'"[24] Instead of "taking" wild animals, stock-breeders raise domestic ones—and to raise them successfully, they need things that cannot be "taken": things like rain, good grass, or protection from wolves. These things can only be given by the ancestors. In return, the ancestors ask for sacrificed domestic animals, conceived of as substitutes for humans. But this repayment is, in effect, made in advance, for the emphasis is on sacrifice as an investment undertaken with an eye to future returns. The sacrifice of animal substitutes for humans is thus associated with what can only be called a change in the temporal orientation of the reciprocity. As Hamayon puts it, "the subjective dynamic that moves the exchange process forward is turned around if compared to the hunter's: for the stock-breeder, it is 'giving' that takes precedence and triggers the process."[25] Hunters take, and the animal spirits take back. Stock-breeders give, and the ancestral spirits give back.

Hunters want the animal spirits to take back as little as possible. They use every trick in the book to get the better of their exchange partners, but they know they are living on borrowed time. However much they manage to minimize or postpone the return payment, all their tricks cannot prevent the moment of reckoning from arriving eventually. They remain locked in a mortal game of negative reciprocity from which they cannot escape. By contrast, the stock-breeders do not content themselves with using trickery to improve their odds within the same framework. Instead, they set out to change the rules of the game. Rather than scheming to put off the inevitable return payment, they reverse the direction of the reciprocity by anticipating the return—and offering it up in advance. After giving to the ancestors through sacrifice, they can *look forward* to the ancestors' giving back. Reciprocation by the exchange partners is no longer feared as in the case of the hunters' vengeance relationship with animals. Sacrifice is the trick that allows stock-breeders to exchange negative for positive reciprocity.

In reality, there are two tricky aspects to the stock-breeder's sacrificing. One is the substitution of animals for human victims. This is a technique for minimizing giving that is comparable, as Hamayon points out, to the hunter's trick of postponement.[26] Like the latter, it is a means of obtaining an advantage within the context of the exchange game as it is played. On the other hand, the aspect of sacrifice that I have underscored, the fact of giving in advance, is not at all comparable to the hunter's trick. Indeed, it is the very opposite of postponement. If it nevertheless works to the stock-breeder's advantage, that is because it operates at a different level—at a metalevel—by turning around the whole dynamic of the exchange process, thus changing the way the game is played. This, I would argue, is quite a sophisticated trick, and one that can only be accomplished through sacrifice.

One could even argue that the same trick lies at the heart of today's market economy. For as remote as religious sacrifice may be from modern commerce, entrepreneurs resemble spirit-worshippers in pursuing their own interest by anticipating the demand of potential exchange partners. Adam Smith's butcher and baker are motivated more by self-interest than benevolence, but the logic of the market requires them to simulate benevolence by gearing their production to their customers' needs, in the same way that stock-breeders simulate benevolence to the ancestors by offering sacrifices while thinking of their own future profits. The hunters, for their part, subordinate self-interest and show real benevolence to fellow humans by sharing their food in a way that stock-breeders and merchants do not, yet they practice negative reciprocity when it comes to their relations with animals.[27] Without sacrifice, they lack the future orientation of the stock-breeders. They do not look forward to a return blow from the animals; they only try to postpone it as long as possible.

The Hunter's Arrow and the Shaman's

Here one might object that even to postpone a return payment, one must be able to see it coming. If the hunters can manipulate the future even to this limited extent without the benefit of sacrifice, where does that leave the claimed association between sacrifice and the anticipation of the return? Before closing, we need to examine more carefully the brand of trickery employed by the hunters. How exactly do they go about trying to get a better deal in their life-exchange with the animals?

It is the job of the shaman to take advantage of the delay between taking and giving back in order to obtain the best possible terms in the exchange relation. Through a collective ritual in which all the group's hunters take part, the shaman must obtain promises of "good luck" for the hunting season from the animal spirits. However, after acquiring these promises, he must let the spirits devour him. "His symbolic self-offering is intended to serve as a token of the group's future repayment to the spirits," Hamayon explains.[28] This ritual would thus seem to accomplish what can only be called a sacrificial substitution of the shaman's person for the members of the community whose lives he is expected to protect. Although the hunters know the animal spirits will take their lives as repayment sooner or later, the shaman is responsible for ensuring that this happens later rather than sooner. He does this in the first place by anticipating the return payment and offering it up in advance by letting the animal spirits feed on his own body.

The ideological primacy of taking among the hunters must therefore be qualified. While they themselves manifest an aggressive ethic of taking, they let their shaman open the hunting season with a ritual that also includes giving. Indeed, since animals are also said to "give themselves," spontaneously meeting the hunter's arrow,[29] the shaman's initial giving of himself reframes the entire hunt as an occasion for the animals to make a return gift. In this way, the shaman's self-sacrifice enables him to give the hunters' negative reciprocity with the animals a positive spin.

There is a trick to the shaman's self-sacrifice, however, for after he is eaten by the animal spirits the participants manage to ritually "revive" him. He then reveals that he has one more trick up his sleeve. According to Hamayon, "The ritual ends with a divinatory sequence where the shaman proceeds to determine the supposed life expectancy of the participants. Some of them may then be marked out for dying soon. Their eventual death will be interpreted in terms of payment to the spirits." Here there is a substitution of some individuals for all the members of the community: in Hamayon's words, it is "necessary that some members die for the group to survive."[30] But more than substitution is involved. Once again, the return payment is anticipated, although it will not be collected until later. Anticipating the return payment by symbolically offering up some hunters in advance is precisely the trick that makes it possible to put off the actual repayment until later.

Putting to death a member of their own group was the trick used by the Chukchi to forestall revenge. Hamayon's Siberian hunters postpone retribution by marking members of their own group for death. If they do not actually kill the designated victims, neither do they actually hope to prevent their exchange partners from striking back in the end. Yet their efforts to modulate the logic of vengeance inevitably lead them to put a sacrificial twist on it, a twist that brings them close to the logic of the gift. A final example will make this clear.

In a Tungus divinatory procedure described by Hamayon,[31] the victims are designated in a way that overtly reverses the ordinary chain of events. Without this ceremony conducted by the shaman, the hunters would be the ones to deal the opening blows, shooting arrows at their prey, and the animals' revenge would follow in the normal course of negative reciprocity. But the shaman opens the hunting season with arrows that point to human victims, allowing the animals, in effect, to savor their vengeance ahead of time. Here is how the trick works. For each participant in the ceremony, the shaman fires a small arrow through a hole in the hut. If it lands far away, the participant still has long years of hunting ahead of him. But if it does not, he has been singled out as a return payment to the hunted—a return payment offered up in advance. Letting the shaman's arrow fall close to home means changing reciprocities.

CHAPTER 3

Trying to Stop the Trojan War

s there a secret to being a successful prophet? Perhaps the trick is to mix prediction and action, as the following Buddhist parable suggests.

A mendicant monk came to a man's house seeking food, and the man asked his wife to give the visitor something to eat. Observing the beauty of the wife, the monk decided to play a joke on the husband. He intoned the following three phrases in oracular fashion: "*Sensual craving; afterwards, misfortune; getting out.*"

Since his host was baffled by this utterance, the monk said, "Let me show you the meaning." He turned to the wife, took her face in his hands, and planted a passionate kiss on her lips. Then he told the husband, "That is *sensual craving.*"

The husband, indignant, grabbed a stick and hit him. But the monk was unperturbed. "That," he explained, "is *afterwards, misfortune.*" At this, the husband became even more indignant and raised his stick to hit him again.

This time, however, the monk ran for the door. Only after clearing the threshold did he turn his head to say, "And that, my good fellow, is *getting out.*"[1]

Some people will go to any length to prove a point. The monk took a risk by deliberately triggering retaliation, but at least he was smart enough to have an exit strategy. As his practical joke reminds us, violence can be as predictable as one-two-three. Since it tends to unfold and escalate in mechanical fashion, it lends itself to manipulation by provocateurs and terrorists who cynically incite the very violence they so righteously denounce.[2]

When he incites the husband to violence by kissing the wife, the monk commits a particularly grievous offense because he is a guest in the other man's house. In traditional societies, the offering and acceptance of hospitality imposes sacred obligations of mutual respect on both host and guest, obligations that the monk blithely flouts in order to make his prophecy come true. It is hard to avoid the feeling that he has cheated by intervening so directly in the course of events. True prophets are content to issue their predictions; they do not take action to influence events themselves. Or do they?

In reality, it is not so easy to unmix prediction from action for, as Jean-Pierre Dupuy emphasizes, the prediction itself is liable to influence the course of events.[3] Dupuy discusses the example of a doomsaying prophet who successfully alerts his listeners to the threat of catastrophe, thus inducing them to change their behavior in such a way as to avert the danger. In this case, the prophecy is self-refuting; its very persuasiveness ends up undermining its accuracy. Dupuy suggests that this paradox is unavoidable: only by imparting ontological force to the predicted catastrophe and inscribing it in the future as an inexorable destiny can the prophet of doom save his listeners from their fate.

Dupuy also mentions a counterexample, that of Cassandra, whose dire predictions all come true. The mythical explanation is that a god has condemned her prophecies to go unheeded, but this deus ex machina may be unnecessary. Even were Cassandra able to impress on her listeners the truth of what she says, I suspect she would still be helpless to save them. The reason has to do with the particular type of catastrophe she predicts. Whereas Dupuy is primarily concerned with ecological disaster, Cassandra's visions of the future are filled with violence and war, and in this case, I would submit, the circular logic plays out differently.[4] The more people hate an enemy for the violence they believe he will inflict on them, the more they will behave in such a way as to incite violence. The more they fear war to be imminent, the more they will act in such a way as to bring war about.

Rather than being self-refuting, then, prophecies of violence and war tend to be self-fulfilling. This is a secret well known to political leaders.

When they want war, one of the actions they take is to present war as inevitable. The more inevitable a war is perceived to be, the more inevitable it becomes. Preparations for battle create their own momentum, and any leader who might want to stand in the way will have a daunting task. It is always easier to provoke violence than to prevent it.

The Symmetry of Reprisals

The difficulty of heading off a war seen as inevitable is the theme of a remarkable 1935 play by French writer Jean Giraudoux, *La guerre de Troie n'aura pas lieu*. The title sentence is also the first line, spoken by Andromache to Cassandra: "The Trojan War will not take place." Cassandra retorts, "I'll make you a bet on it." The rest of the two-act play imagines the desperate efforts of Andromache and her husband, the Trojan champion Hector, to prevent a war the spectator knows to be inevitable. But why was it inevitable?

We all remember how the war began, or at least we think we do: the Trojan prince Paris provoked the Greeks by carrying off Menelaus's wife Helen, entranced by the face that was to launch a thousand ships. We seldom think to ask what Paris was doing on the Greeks' turf in the first place. In fact, Paris's father, the Trojan king Priam, had sent him to Greece at the head of a great fleet of Trojan ships to demand the return of Priam's sister Hesione, whom the Greek hero Hercules had carried off years before. A revisionist historian from Troy would doubtless credit Hesione with having first set the ships in motion. If Hercules had not abducted Hesione, Paris would never have eloped with Helen. From the Trojan point of view, then, Paris was merely turning the tables on the Greeks, and the massive Greek counterstrike appears unjustified. From the Greek point of view, however, it would be quite unfair to blame Hercules for provoking the conflict, for he had previously suffered treacherous treatment at the hands of Hesione's father and thus had every right to avenge himself . . .

And so it goes. The forgotten backstory to the Trojan war illustrates the way in which a chain of reprisals tends to perpetuate itself. As we saw earlier, the problem is that the parties to a conflict do not "punctuate" the sequence of events in the same fashion. What one side sees as just retribution for a previous offense, the other side will see as a new offense calling for just retribution. Since the parties disagree on where the sequence began, they cannot agree on where it should end. As long as each side tries to have the last word, the violence never comes to a full stop. Each party looks backward to what the other party did, and the conflict hurtles inexorably forward, seemingly propelled by some mysterious force that eludes the grasp of ordinary mortals. When Paris sets sail for Greece, only Cassandra is able to predict that his expedition will bring disaster to Troy.

Let us now pick up the chain of events at the traditional starting point. Once Paris encounters Helen and carries her with him to Troy, the stage is set for war with Greece. The offense committed by Paris is all the more serious in that he had been welcomed as a guest in Menelaus's house. Stealing his host's wife was a poor way of repaying his hospitality. As in our Buddhist fable, the aggrieved husband reacts with predictable violence. Determined to hit back as hard as possible, he gathers his allies and their armies and heads for Troy. Giraudoux's play begins after Paris's *sensual craving* has brought about this *misfortune*, and the problem facing the hero of the drama, Hector, is that of *getting out*. Can he find a way out of a sequence of events that seems fated to end in war?

Giraudoux's Hector is a professional warrior who has grown tired of fighting. He vividly recalls the day that "job fatigue" overwhelmed him just as he was bending over a fallen enemy of his own age in order to finish him off: "In the past, those I was going to kill had seemed to me to be the opposite of myself. This time I found myself kneeling over a mirror. The death I was going to mete out was a little suicide."[5] Killing his enemy was like killing himself inasmuch as his enemy was his own mirror image. Thanks to this sudden insight, Hector is able to transcend his previous belief that his enemies were somehow his opposites.

When violence is at its height, opposition seems to be greatest, and yet the adversaries behave in the same way, each intent on killing the other because the other is intent on killing him. The illusion of difference is accompanied by a structural symmetry that usually goes unperceived. The intuition expressed by Giraudoux's Hector corresponds to the lesson that René Girard has drawn from his studies of Greek tragedy: "Conflict feeds on symmetry and it renders symmetry ever more exact."[6] The more fiercely the adversaries attack each other, the more closely they come to resemble one another. "The end result of the struggle is the stupid reciprocity of reprisals between undifferentiated antagonists," comments Girard.[7]

Behind the epic grandeur of Homeric warriors, the reciprocity of undifferentiated antagonists is visible. At the heart of the *Iliad* is the opposition between Hector and the Greek champion, Achilles. The decisive combat between the two is long-delayed, however, because Achilles' resentment against the leader of his own side, Agamemnon, causes him to hold back from fighting on behalf of the Greeks. Agamemnon angers Achilles by appropriating a female captive that Achilles had claimed as a prize for himself. To the extent that this conflict within the Greek camp mirrors the conflict over Helen that triggered the war against the Trojans, it already suggests an underlying resemblance between the two sides. If the Greek leader's behavior is not unlike that of Paris, it is hard to single out the Trojans as the villains, and Achilles tells Agamemnon as much: "It was not the spearmen of Troy who caused me to come here and fight—I have no quarrel with them. . . . And now you even threaten to take away my prize yourself."[8]

While Achilles stubbornly refuses to battle the Trojans, he eventually consents to send his bosom friend Patroclus to fight in his stead, garbed in his own armor. Patroclus accomplishes many feats of valor against the Trojans, who mistake him for the famed warrior whose armor he wears. But Hector succeeds in killing Patroclus and seizes the armor as a prize or trophy, donning it himself. The death of Patroclus causes Achilles to enter the fray at last, determined to avenge his friend. When Achilles finally kills the Trojan champion, his vengeance falls upon an adversary who is clad in his own armor: Hector is a mirror image of Achilles. But Patroclus was already a mirror image of Achilles when Hector killed him. A chain of violent reprisals reproduces the same scene again and again. Like Gjorg at the end of Ismail Kadare's novel *Broken April*, each killer is destined to be killed in his turn. Before Patroclus dies, he prophesies the death of Hector, and before Hector dies, he prophesies the death of Achilles. As the words of Giraudoux's Hector suggest, the death each metes out is also a suicide: by killing his adversary he seals his own fate.

In Giraudoux's play, Hector wants at all costs to avoid a suicidal war with Greece. He therefore seeks to persuade the Greek ambassador, Ulysses, that the Greeks should simply take back Helen and forget the affront committed by Paris. His hope is that, if Ulysses does not want war any more than he does, then the war will not take place. But when he puts the question to Ulysses directly—"Do you want war?"—the answer is less than satisfying: "I do not want it. But I am not so sure what its intentions are."[9] The Greek ambassador thus treats war as if it were, in Dupuy's terminology, a "quasi-subject," emerging from the interaction of the human protagonists, but endowed with a will of its own: an independent force beyond human control, analogous to fate or destiny. If the outcome is up to fate, it matters little whether Hector and Ulysses want war; the war will take place if it is destined to do so.

As readers or spectators of Giraudoux's play, we belong to a later generation coming after the catastrophe supposed to have befallen Troy. Projecting ourselves back into Hector's present from our privileged position in the future, we know that Cassandra is right: the war will take place. Her prophecy coincides with our memory. From her point of view, the events we remember are future events; from our point of view, her foreknowledge of these events is like a memory of the future. Dupuy has suggested that prophecy always amounts to summoning up a memory of events to come.[10] In Giraudoux's play, Cassandra is not the only prophet: Helen also has visions of the future. She describes her own visions and those of Cassandra in terms that correspond strikingly to Dupuy's temporal metaphysics: "Our advantage is that our visions fuse with our memories, the future with the past!"[11]

The peculiar properties of Helen's vision seemingly extend to lovers as well as events. When pressed by Hector, she admits that Paris has begun to fade in her eyes: the men who wait upon her in the present stand out less clearly in her field of vision than those whom she awaits.[12] Pushing her to abandon Paris and let her countrymen take her back home, Hector asks: "Well then, between this return to a Greece that is not disagreeable to you, and the terrible catastrophe of war, would you hesitate to choose?" Hector's question presupposes what Dupuy calls our ordinary or common-sense metaphysics, which envisages time as branching off into forking paths, each equally open to us, between which we are free to choose.[13] But Helen's answer repudiates the idea of a choice between equally possible options. In the following excerpts from her dialogue with Hector, she evokes a more paradoxical metaphysics in which her present choices are determined by the future events she foresees as taking place:

HELEN: You don't understand me at all, Hector. I don't hesitate to
  choose. It would be too easy to say "I'll do this," or "I'll do that"
  for this or that to take place. . . . I choose [the events] that are not
  shadows to me. I choose the ones I see.
HECTOR: . . . Do you see the battle?
HELEN: Yes.
HECTOR: And the city crumbles or burns, isn't that right?
HELEN: Yes. It's bright red. . . .
HECTOR : . . . But we need peace.
HELEN: I don't see peace.[14]

If Hector ultimately fails to stop the topless towers of Ilium from burning,
it is because nobody succeeds in seeing peace, whereas everyone can see the
battle.

Even the war's opponents have trouble believing it is not destined to
occur. This is the implication of the phrase "the Trojan War will not take
place." If this phrase were found only in the title, it could be interpreted as
no more than an ironic wink at the modern audience: from our privileged
vantage point, we know the statement to be wrong. But, as noted earlier, the
same words are pronounced by Andromache in the opening line of the play:
"The Trojan War will not take place, Cassandra!" Rather than merely asserting that there will be no war with Greece, Andromache refers to the "Trojan
War" as if it were something that already existed, paradoxically endowing
this future event with an ontological weight it should not yet possess.

Thus, while ostensibly contradicting Cassandra's prophecy that the war
is fated to occur, Andromache herself takes the prophesied war as her reference point. Once the war does occur, it becomes all the easier to believe that
it was indeed fated to do so, even though the shared sense that it was fated
to do so may have been one of the very things that caused the war to occur in
the first place. As I suggested earlier, belief in the inevitability of war may be
a self-fulfilling prophecy. Is it possible to imagine a self-fulfilling prophecy
capable of preventing a war from occurring?

Once, when Giraudoux's play was staged in Bad-Wurtemberg, would-be
spectators arriving at the theater saw a poster at the entrance announcing, in
two lines of unequal height:

THE TROJAN WAR
WILL NOT TAKE PLACE

Everybody turned around and left, convinced that the performance had been cancelled.[15] This incident calls to mind a popular slogan of the Vietnam-era peace movement: What if they gave a war and nobody came? Unfortunately, a war is not as easy to cancel as a theatrical production. If Giraudoux is right, war cannot be averted as long as people are unable to *see* peace. Perhaps, then, a self-fulfilling prophecy of a different kind is needed, one that involves envisioning peaceful relations. To find an example of such a prophecy, we must leave Giraudoux and return to Homer.

Exchanging Armor Instead of Spears

One of the most intriguing minor episodes of the *Iliad* takes place in book 6 when two warriors meet on the battlefield and decide not to fight. Marcel Mauss observes that laying down the spear is the first condition for peaceful exchange. Homer inverts Mauss's dictum by portraying the anticipation of peaceful exchange as the first condition for laying down the spear.

Before facing Glaukos in single combat, Diomedes, the grandson of Oineus, asks, "Which of mortal men are you, my friend?" Glaukos answers by recounting the history of his family, revealing himself to be the grandson of Bellerophontes. Upon learning this, Diomedes plants his spear in the ground and joyously replies:

> Well then, you are a guest-friend of mine from far back in our families! Godlike Oineus once entertained the excellent Bellerophontes in his house, and kept him for twenty days; and they also gave each other fine gifts of friendship. . . . So now you have me as your loyal host in the heart of Argos, and I have you in Lycia, whenever I come to that country. Let us keep away from each other's spears, even in the thick of the fighting. There are many of the Trojans and their famous allies for me to kill . . . and again many of the Achaians for you to cut down, all those you can. And let us exchange armour with each other, so the others too can see that we are proud to claim guest-friendship from our fathers' time.[16]

The hospitality given by Oineus to Bellerophontes and the "fine gifts" they exchanged sealed an alliance destined to perpetuate itself from one generation to the next. Not only does Diomedes propose to renew this alliance through an exchange of gifts between himself and Glaukos, but he suggests that the transition from warlike to peaceful relations is a matter of substituting one form of reciprocity for another: "Let us keep away from each other's spears. . . . And let us exchange armor with each other." If combat is a form of negative reciprocity in which each party hurls his spear at the other, then the most logical way to avoid fighting is through the positive reciprocity of an exchange in which each offers his armor to the other.

It is possible to identify several layers of meaning in this exchange. Since a warrior's armor shields him from the blows of his enemies, an exchange of armor amounts to a mutual defense pact. At the same time, since armor houses the warrior in a protective shell, offering one's armor may also be seen as the battlefield equivalent of offering hospitality. Just as Diomedes' grandfather offered hospitality to Glaukos's grandfather, Diomedes offers his armor to Glaukos, thereby initiating a new exchange of particularly fine gifts. Few possessions are more valuable to a Homeric warrior than his dazzling armor forged from bronze or gold.

In order to appreciate fully the significance of this exchange, however, we must take into account the importance of armor as a trophy that one warrior strives to wrest from another. We saw earlier how the back-and-forth movements of Achilles' armor mark the successive stages of his conflict with Hector. When Hector kills Patroclus, he takes from him the armor that came from Achilles, and when Achilles kills Hector, he takes from him the armor that came from Patroclus. Each move seems designed to undo the previous move.

The use of Patroclus as a stand-in for Achilles is a masterful narrative device. It makes it possible for the circle of vengeance to close entirely upon itself. First Hector kills Achilles in the guise of his surrogate, then Achilles kills Hector. Each gets his revenge, but at the price of his own life. Is there any way out of such a vicious circle?

The same narrative device puts us on the right track. Everything takes place as if, before killing Hector to take his armor, Achilles had sent him his own armor on the shoulders of his friend, thus offering him his revenge in advance. Couldn't one imagine a scenario in which each offers his armor in advance without waiting for the other to take it from him?

That is precisely the scenario imagined by Diomedes. "Let us exchange armor with each other," he tells Glaukos. Let each of us offer his armor to the other in advance, without waiting to kill or be killed. Each will surrender the coveted trophy to the other; neither will surrender his life.

Two distinct exchanges are superimposed here. The first, in which each gives the other a trophy, is conventionally premised on a remembered past exchange in which each warrior's forebear offered the other's forebear "gifts of friendship": "Let us exchange armor with each other, so the others too can see that we are proud to claim guest-friendship from our fathers' time." But the second exchange, in which each allows the other to keep his life, is based on a prophesied *future* exchange of hospitality between the warriors themselves: "So now you have me as your loyal host in the heart of Argos, and I have you in Lycia, whenever I come to that country."

Diomedes weaves seamlessly back and forth between a memory of the past and what we might well call a "memory" of the future. He refers to the future exchange between Glaukos and himself as if it possessed the same certainty as the past exchange between their forebears. This allows the prophesied future exchange to serve as the premise for the proposed present exchange. But the very possibility of the future exchange depends on carrying out the action that he derives from it: "Let us keep away from each other's spears." If one were to take the other's life today, he could not receive his hospitality tomorrow. The future transaction is at once the product and the premise of the present one; as in Dupuy's metaphysics, a causal loop of mutual determination appears to make time circular, or to collapse it into an eternal present: "Now you have me as your host in Argos, and I have you in Lycia."

By making the future present, Diomedes helps Glaukos to *see* it. Rather than proclaiming "the battle between us will not take place," or urging his adversary to choose peace, he *shows* him what their peaceful relationship will look like. The more real he can make this future seem to the other, the more likely it is to become a reality. If the announcement of a peaceful exchange tomorrow succeeds in preventing a battle today, then it functions as a self-fulfilling prophecy.

I argued previously that the transition from violence to peaceful exchange entails a reversal in temporal orientation. Where the negative reciprocity of vengeance looks backward to the past violence it attempts to cancel out, the positive reciprocity of gift-giving looks forward to the peaceful relations it aims to produce. Instead of killing the person who was the last to kill, one gives to the person who will be the next to give. Diomedes gives his armor to the person who will give him hospitality in Lycia; Glaukos gives his armor to the person who will be his host in the heart of Argos. In positive reciprocity, one anticipates the desire of the other party and gives them what they want in advance.

This in a sense is what Hector tries to do by giving Helen back to the Greeks. "We'll return her," he tells Ulysses, "and you'll guarantee peace. No more reprisals, no more vengeance."[17] To be sure, returning Helen is not the same as making a gift, and Hector has no positive vision of peace, defining it simply as the absence of violence. At first, however, his strategy seems to work. Ulysses agrees to accept Helen and go. It looks as if the Trojan War will not take place—until something happens at the last minute that changes everything, proving once more the relevance of Marcel Mauss's observations on the fundamental "instability" between peaceful exchange and war.

Just as Ulysses and his party are heading back to their ship, a drunken Greek straggler staggers by and ogles Andromache. Overcome with sensual craving, he kisses her right in front of Hector, who slowly raises his spear to strike him. Will Hector react as mechanically as the offended husband in our Buddhist parable, even at the cost of derailing the fragile peace agreement?

Giraudoux has placed Hector in a position comparable to that of Menelaus. After maintaining that the offense committed by Paris against Helen's husband is not reason enough for war, he now finds himself in the insulted husband's shoes. If he responds to the provocation by killing the drunken Greek, the latter's countrymen will feel obliged to avenge his death, and Hector will himself have started the war he has spent the rest of the play trying to stop. Through a mighty exertion of willpower, he manages to contain his fury. The drunken Greek begins to leave, and Hector slowly lowers his spear. Reason and the will to peace have seemingly prevailed. It still looks as if the Trojan War will not take place.

Then a fellow Trojan bursts on the scene and berates Hector for surrendering Helen. This character is a comic figure, a self-important patriotic poet who has been clamoring for war throughout the play. Now he shouts for the Trojans to take up their arms, announcing proudly that he has written them a battle hymn. Hector can no longer contain himself. "Here is for your battle hymn," he says, and fells the poet with his spear. Having removed this last obstacle to peace, he assures Andromache the war will not take place.[18]

Meanwhile, the other Trojans arrive and find the poet on the ground. Before he dies, he tells them it was the drunken Greek who struck him, whereupon the enraged Trojans chase after the Greek and kill him. Now his countrymen will feel obliged to avenge his death. The war will take place, just as Cassandra had said it would.

How are we to interpret this final turn of events? On a first reading, it would seem to confirm that, one way or another, the war was destined to occur. Despite his best efforts, Hector was powerless to stop it. He was no match for fate.

Yet Hector did not merely fail to stop the war. However indirectly and inadvertently, he triggered it through his own violence. After restraining himself from striking the Greek who kissed his wife, he vented his fury on the Trojan who had been a thorn in his side right along. In effect, rather than suppressing his violent impulse entirely, he diverted it from an external enemy to an internal opponent. It is difficult not to see the murder of the poet as the substitution of one victim for another: in René Girard's terms, a sacrificial displacement of violence.

Such sacrificial displacement is extremely common. It is visible even in the episode from the *Iliad* that we just examined. After telling Glaukos, "Let us keep away from each other's spears," Diomedes hastens to add: "There are many of the Trojans . . . for me to kill [and] many of the Achaians for you to cut down," as if the targeting of surrogate victims will allow each of them to satisfy vicariously his urge to kill the other. A similar idea appears in Giraudoux's play when Andromache praises hunting as a viable substitute for warfare: "Every time I have seen a stag or an eagle killed, I have offered it my thanks. I knew it was dying for Hector."[19]

Sacrificial displacement often proves an effective means of controlling violence. Indeed, as we shall soon see, the displacement of collective violence onto a surrogate victim could well be at the very origin of social order. Yet Girard has noted that the displacement process can backfire: "Being continuous in both directions, the chain of substitution may at any time reverse itself."[20] This is what happens after Hector kills the Trojan poet instead of the Greek drunkard: by blaming the latter for his death, the Trojan succeeds in redirecting the violence back toward the Greek. But it was Hector who first unleashed the violence when he threw the spear at his warmongering countryman.

The more I hate war, Hector remarks in his last conversation with Ulysses, the more I am possessed by an "irrepressible desire to kill."[21] These words turn out to be prophetic. They explain the outcome better than all the talk of fate or destiny. Too often what we call fate is only the mechanics of human hate.

When individuals are caught up in a process of interaction that runs out of control and produces a result they did not seek, it is easy to imagine that some powerful force has thwarted their will. Such a force exists: it is nothing other than the dynamic emerging from the interaction process itself and sweeping each individual along in its wake. We will see next how the belief in an all-powerful god can be born of such a collective dynamic.

PART 2

Self-Transcendence

CHAPTER 4

Return to the Beginning, or the Making of a Metagod

H ow do you make a god? Does it take a miracle? What kind of miracle? We are going to examine a series of myths from ancient India that reveal what the gods themselves do when they need to conjure up a metagod. But first, let us listen to a legend reported by contemporary French anthropologist Olivier Herrenschmidt. He calls it an "edifying story" about days gone by.

Some young children decide to play at making a sacrifice to the goddess Bangaramma. First they fashion a knife out of clay, which they allow to dry for four days. On the fifth day one of them plays the goat. His companions tie a garland of leaves around his neck, bind him to a rope, and lead him to the temple. There they present him ceremoniously to the goddess, at which point, Herrenschmidt tells us, the child playing the goat is "properly—and miraculously—decapitated."[1]

There is a curious disconnect between the beginning and the end of this story. When the children decide to play at sacrifice, the first thing they do is make a knife. Then they let several days pass in order to be absolutely sure the knife is ready for use before leading the victim to the altar. At the last moment, however, the victim loses his head "miraculously," with no muss or fuss, and all talk of knives is forgotten.

What is the moral of this tale? It brings to mind another story in which children play at sacrifice and their games take a deadly turn. In William Golding's novel *Lord of the Flies*, British schoolboys marooned on a desert island are terrified of an unseen presence in the darkness that they call "the Beast." To lift their spirits, the boys go hunting for pigs, and when they kill a pig they offer its head to the Beast. Sometimes they merely play at hunting, and one of the boys plays the pig. One night the game gets out of hand. They dance round and round in a Durkheimian frenzy of collective effervescence, until, Golding writes, "there was the throb and stamp of a single organism."[2] When the dance is over, one boy, who had the misfortune to stumble into the middle of the circle, is dead.

Who killed the dead boy? In the Indian legend, the child's death is a miracle. None of the children is responsible; the goddess brings the sacrifice to completion herself. Golding's novel deconstructs the miracle. None of the children is responsible because the sacrifice is carried out by the group as a whole. Since the group acts unanimously, no individual is responsible—only the divinity is. But the divinity of the group is, as Émile Durkheim would have it, none other than the group itself. In this sense, the divinity is real enough. As one of Golding's boys says, "maybe there is a beast . . . maybe it's only us."[3] When the crowd dances in unison like a single organism, it becomes the Beast. It creates the divinity out of itself through an act of self-transcendence.[4] The moral of the story is that if enough excitable individuals all pitch in together, making a god is child's play.

Golding's children conjure up a god as a means of self-organization in the absence of adults. As Italian political philosopher Luigi Alfieri observes, "The fact that these are children who, without guides or models, in a savage, primitive context resembling the state of nature, confront the problem of giving life to an organized community, should make us view Golding's novel as a sort of conceptual experiment on the *very origin* of the political phenomenon. And," he adds, "in this imaginary return to the beginning of politics, the encounter with violence is inevitable."[5]

Let us now turn to an Indian myth that addresses the same problem of how to organize a community while depicting the process of god-creation in amazingly explicit terms. The only thing missing, apparently, is the encounter with violence. Charles Malamoud, the leading French authority on Vedic religion, calls this myth "the contractual body of the gods." He sees in it a parable of how the "political bond in the pure state" is formed. Although it takes place during one of the recurrent battles between the gods and their demonic foes, the Asuras, this external rivalry serves only as a backdrop. Like the Greek camp at the opening of the *Iliad*, the camp of the Vedic gods is beset by conflict. Unless they can overcome their internal divisions, the gods cannot hope to vanquish their external enemies. The real theme of the myth is the need to assure peace among the gods themselves. Here is the most concise version furnished by Malamoud:

> The gods and Asuras were in conflict. The gods were divided. Not wanting to accept the superiority of one over another, they separated into five groups. . . . They reflected: "Our enemies, the Asuras, are benefitting from our division. Let us levy from each of us and put together in a deposit these bodies which are dear to us. From these bodies he shall be separated, the one who is the first among us to show himself hostile to another."[6]

This myth has often been compared to a social contract theory, and it is easy to see why. But as Malamoud rightly emphasizes,[7] the myth does not provide a model for the real Indian social organization, which is characterized by a caste hierarchy. The origin of the Indian caste system is described by another, better-known myth found in the *Rig Veda*. In this other myth the social organization is traced back to the sacrificial dismemberment of a primordial man: the elite Brahmins are born from his head, the warrior caste from his arms, and so on.[8] Moreover, traditional Indian society truly is organized around sacrifice. It is based on the ritual functions of the different castes—on how these different human groups relate to the gods.[9]

Our myth of the gods' compact is not concerned with this social organization; it has another function. It is invoked to explain a special preliminary ritual used to establish confidence among the human beings who must cooperate with each other in the process of carrying out a sacrifice.[10] For if the social contract is founded on sacrifice, we still need to know what sacrifice is founded upon. In other words, we need a metamyth, the myth of the metaritual on which the success of the sacrificial ritual depends. And this metamyth must therefore show how the social bond can be formed without the benefit of ritual sacrifice.

Now, the gods of our myth face the same problem of organizing themselves without recourse to sacrifice. Why? Quite simply, because, being gods, they have no one else to sacrifice *to*.[11] What they need is a metagod. Left to themselves, the gods are in the same predicament as Golding's children abandoned on a desert island with no adults to act as guides or models.

The problem is the political one of arbitration among equals. How do you surmount the divisions that arise when nobody wants to accept the superiority of one individual over another? The answer is for each individual to recognize the superiority of the higher-order entity formed by all of them together. This solution is realized in the myth by having each individual god renounce the most precious part of himself and hand it over to an external being composed of nothing other than the sum of all the individual parts. In this way the arbitration is accomplished by the collectivity as a whole. The myth describes the unanimous action through which the collectivity transcends itself. Durkheim would be pleased. If the god of the group is the group itself, the metagod is the group of gods itself.

However, Malamoud provides a second version of the myth in which a quite different figure is elevated to the status of metagod:

> The gods, incapable of getting along, separated into four groups. Taking advantage of their discord, their enemies, the Asuras and Raksasas [another type of demon], slipped among them. The gods decided to make an agreement. "Let us cede to the pre-eminence of one among us." It is Indra that they designated as their leader.[12]

At first it would appear that we might have to revise our hypothesis. The metagod is not the group as a whole this time; it is a single individual chosen from within the group: Indra. The text goes on to identify Indra as the depositary of the precious bodies that the other gods must sever from themselves and pool together. The procedure is thus the same as in the first version, except that Indra takes the place of the collectivity.

The choice of Indra for the prime role is not unexpected since he traditionally figures in Indian mythology as the king of the gods. Still, we might want to push our inquiry further. After all, it is a little surprising that the same gods who only a moment ago were unable to acknowledge anyone's superiority should now so suddenly rally around Indra. How did he get to be king?

The choice of a king is no easy task. "Whom shall we choose as ruler of a state?" asks Blaise Pascal. "The most virtuous and able man? That sets us straightaway at daggers drawn, with everyone claiming to be the most virtuous and able."[13] The gods in our myth were already at daggers drawn when the story opened, even before deciding they should recognize the preeminence of one among them. We need to know how they managed to overcome their divisions and all unite around Indra. What set him above the rest? Who is this Indra, anyway?

"Indra, in truth, is he who burns up yonder," the brahmanic text explains.[14] In other words, Indra is the sun. Now, that makes everything more understandable, doesn't it? No wonder Indra was able to outshine the others. No wonder he was unanimously seen to display the radiance of a king. Hasn't the sun always ruled the skies? There is no more familiar figure in early theories of religion than the sun god. And a sun god would seem to constitute a prototypically external form of transcendence—what Jean-Pierre Dupuy would call an "exogenous fixed point."[15] A sun god is not an emergent phenomenon. Or is it?

The myth quickly throws us for a loop by specifying that "to be sure, [Indra] did not burn at the origin." To be sure: for it is only "by this energy (derived from the divine bodies deposited with him) that he burns."[16] Thus, Indra is the sun, but—and this makes all the difference from our viewpoint—the sun owes its radiance to the combined contributions of all the individual gods that go to make it up.

A third variant of the myth spells this process out even more clearly:

> The gods, none of them submitting to the authority of any of the others, separated into four groups. Then they constituted a common bloc of well-loved bodies which they levied from each of them and which they deposited in the sun up yonder. "That is why the sun burns so ardently."[17]

This version seemingly cuts to the chase by skipping any mention of Indra and sending the levied bodies directly up yonder, where they cause the sun to burn. But the sun's status is once again problematic. Although the text refers to it as if it were a purely external entity that already existed from the beginning, it also suggests there was a time when the sun did not yet burn. But a sun that does not yet burn is not yet the sun. The assertion that the gods deposited their well-loved bodies "*in* the sun" can only be the fruit of a retrospective illusion. What the myth actually describes is the origin of the sun.

We see more and more clearly how the very act of combining the contributions of the individual divinities produces, in purely *en*dogenous fashion, the transcendence of the metagod. The first, most rationalistic version of the myth points to this truth by limiting itself to describing the collective process at work while leaving Indra and the sun out of the picture entirely. This version features no transcendent entity other than the combined mass of the bodies levied from all the individuals together.

In the second version of the myth, the higher-order entity constituted by all the individuals together is associated with a single one of their number, Indra, and Indra in turn is equated with the sun. This version is no doubt the most complete. It evokes the need to single one individual out from the rest, it locates him squarely at the nexus of all the others' bodies put together, and it lets us glimpse his subsequent transfiguration into a solar divinity.

The third version operates a sort of short circuit between the pooling of all the individual gods' bodies and the birth of the metagod. The latter's apotheosis has become so absolute that no one recalls he started life as one individual among many. Yet a shadowy trace of that individual's presence survives in the suggestion that there was a time when the sun did not yet burn. Before he began to burn, the one who was to become the sun shone no brighter than his fellows. But once he begins to blaze with the energy that comes from being the embodiment of the collectivity, his blinding radiance makes everyone forget his humble origins.

By placing these three variants of the myth side by side, we are able to witness the progressive emergence of collective self-transcendence. The pooling of individual contributions described in the first version is what transfigures the individual member of the group identified by the second version into the wholly external, celestial entity of the third. Taken together, the three narratives form an extraordinary record of the process by which an endogenous fixed point is transformed into an apparently exogenous one.

·   ·   ·

It is hard to think of a fixed point more exogenous—less dependent for its existence on human action—than the sun. Yet it would be wrong to suppose that community rituals aimed at mastering the sun or other external forces of nature are entirely futile. Such rituals may end up accomplishing an endogenous transformation of the community itself. As the anthropologist A. M. Hocart put it, "the early pioneers of thought" succeeded to some extent in "solving the eternal problem of the weather . . . not in the way they thought by controlling the forces of nature, but by controlling themselves and by presenting a more united front."[18] René Girard has suggested how the two things are related: "When men no longer live in harmony with one another, the sun still shines and the rain falls, to be sure, but the fields are less well tended, the harvests less abundant."[19] We saw earlier how Albanian mountain feuds cause fields to lie fallow. When blood flows, the rain may fall on barren land.

The theories of Hocart and Girard both bring into play particular forms of self-transcendence. For Hocart, it is the transcendence or autonomy of men's self-mastery in relation to their own will: this self-mastery is not sought by design, for its own sake; rather, it emerges as an unintended by-product of the quest to control nature, a quest that in Hocart's view motivates the ritual organization of archaic societies. Actions that are meant to control an external entity, the natural environment, end up producing humanity's self-mastery as a system effect. Similarly, for Girard, humanity's self-mastery—in other words, the social order—emerges as a system effect out of actions meant to control, not quite an external entity this time, but rather an internal element that has been externalized or expelled: namely, the surrogate victim. The Durkheimian self-transcendence of society becomes in Girard's conception the self-transcendence of violence. The violence of the group directed against a victim is transformed into the external violence of a divinity that is terrifying, yet benevolent: benevolent inasmuch as it also brings reconciliation.

Now, while the myth we have just analyzed attributes the origin of the sun and of the social order to a process of self-transcendence, this process seems to unfold without violence, as the result of a peaceful agreement. Indeed, the myth hardly exemplifies *spontaneous* self-transcendence in the way it resolves the primordial, Hobbesian political dilemma of arbitration among equals. The reason is that the political solution is achieved by design. In this regard our Indian myth does resemble Western social contract theories. Such theories are in a sense the founding myths of those societies that have sought to free themselves from precisely the kind of ritual organization which, as Malamoud reminds us, characterizes the traditional Indian social system.

The Indian myth tells us that the gods "reflected" on the danger of their divisions and that they "decided to make an agreement." They deliberately undertook to organize themselves. This kind of intentional self-organization is actually the opposite of what is meant by the term "self-organization" in theorizing about emergent systems.[20] What we have instead is a community organizing itself according to a rational plan, as is imagined in social contract theories. Now, theories of the latter type share a common flaw: if humans were really able to come to such an agreement so easily, there would be no problem to solve in the first place. Everybody would already get along. There is thus a mythical circularity at work in such theories that resembles the circularity visible in the second version of the myth, where the metagod is identified with a god who was already there from the beginning: Indra, the king of the gods. How could the gods agree on the preeminence of Indra if none of them would submit to the authority of any other? Girard's idea that the victim is prior to the king is grounded in the simple premise that it is easier to pick a victim than a king. But there is no victim in this myth, only reflection and agreement. Far from behaving like the unruly children in *Lord of the Flies*, the gods comport themselves like the sensible grown-ups whose authoritative presence Golding's youthful protagonists so sorely miss. "They wouldn't quarrel," the children in the novel exclaim wistfully. "They'd meet and have tea and discuss."[21]

Before we conclude that the Vedic gods resolved their differences around a nice pot of hot tea, we might want to look a little more carefully at the first version of the myth. Does it really betray no trace of a victim? Let us return to the last sentence, the one that comes right after the description of the mutual depositing by the gods of the bodies they hold dear: "From these bodies he shall be separated, the one who is the first among us to show himself hostile to another." Now, what does it mean for someone to be separated from part of his corporeal being? Is there not at least a hint of violence here?

In the second version of the myth, the language is even more threatening: "Let him be sent far from us, dispersed, the one among us who would transgress this pact."[22] Of course, the reference here is not to the origin of the pact, but to the enforcement of a pact that already exists. Once again, though, we should recall that Indra is also presented as preexisting the process that generates him. Is it not possible that, through a similar mythic circularity, the violence that punishes the transgressor was already present at the origin to compel the gods to renounce the bodies they held dear?

In the first version of the myth, the formulation of the threat contains a clue that would tend to support this hypothesis. Rather than referring simply to "the one" who would transgress the pact, it specifically singles out "the *first* among us to show himself hostile to another." The notion of a first transgressor is typical of origin myths. Here it is not even a question of the first to transgress the pact, but of the first to show himself hostile.

Such a vaguely worded charge would never pass muster in a modern court. Should someone be punished for a curt word or a dirty look? And how would it be possible to identify the first offender? That is like asking who started a conflict—it takes us back to the "punctuation" problem we discussed before. When hostilities arise, it is generally difficult to determine who showed himself hostile first. This is all the more true when it comes to a group whose members are, as the myth tells us, "incapable of getting along." Could that all be the fault of one individual? A further variant cited by Malamoud refers to "the one who would try to bring trouble among them."[23] Certainly, if they can't get along with each other they are bound to experience trouble, and it will be tempting to find someone on whom to pin the blame. They won't even have to show that the unlucky party actually brought trouble, merely that he "tried" to do so.

This time the crime is, if possible, even more poorly defined. Anybody who does anything that rubs anyone else the wrong way could be accused of trying to make trouble. And how could he defend himself against such a charge? If he seeks to refute his accusers, he is liable to find himself trapped in an insidious catch-22, for the more vociferously he protests his innocence, the more he will look like a troublemaker to those who believe him guilty. Getting rid of such an exasperating individual will naturally seem like a good way to restore peace. Why shouldn't they all pitch in together to teach him a lesson? There will always be time for a tea party later, after things calm down and everyone is in a better mood.

In short, it is not hard to imagine a scenario in which the gods might have sealed their pact by banishing the first suspected "troublemaker" or even "dispersing" him in little pieces. When they found themselves at daggers drawn, with none willing to submit to another, uniting around a victim would surely be easier than choosing a king. Indeed, if we are to believe Hocart—who concluded on the basis of a systematic comparison of installation and funeral ceremonies that "the first kings must have been dead kings"²⁴—then uniting around a victim *was* the "royal road" to choosing a king.²⁵

We noted earlier that our Indian myth is meant to demonstrate how the social bond can be formed without the benefit of ritual sacrifice. Perhaps the compact of the gods is not founded on ritual sacrifice because it is in reality founded on a *non*ritual murder—or a lynching of the type that Girard holds sacrifice to be founded upon. Perhaps the "contractual body of the gods," like Jean-Jacques Rousseau's social contract in Robert Hamerton-Kelly's analysis, displays a "trace of this resolution" of a violent crisis through collective scapegoating.²⁶

Perhaps, but this is pure conjecture. The myth does not come out and say things happened that way. For our hypothesis to be completely persuasive, we would want to find a Vedic myth that explicitly depicts the punishment of a transgressor—the collective violence wrought upon the first to cause trouble by refusing to renounce a body that is dear to him. Such a myth exists. It is the story of how Prajapati comes to be punished for his incestuous refusal to renounce the body of his daughter.

Now, Prajapati is no ordinary malefactor. He is the "Lord of Creatures," the primordial father, the one who, by himself, engendered all the other members of the community. In a word, he is just the kind of metagod we've been looking for, and in normal circumstances he would surely command unquestioning respect. Unfortunately, Prajapati's behavior ill befits his lofty status. By coupling with his own daughter, he arouses the ire of the other gods. They are determined to cut him down to size, but what power do mere street-level deities possess against the Lord of Creatures? As one might guess, it will take a metagod to break a metagod.

Let us turn without further ado to Charles Malamoud's rendering of this new myth:

> Outraged by the incestuous passion that drove Prajapati to pursue his daughter, the Dawn, the other gods sought among them who would be capable of punishing him. No one was up to this task. Therefore they levied, each from his own person, those of their bodies that were most terrifying, and they made these into a single mass that became Rudra; he

it was who would have the strength and cruelty necessary to transpierce Prajapati, and he would specialize in the violent part of the sacrifice, and notably in the wound inflicted on the victim's body by the carver's knife.[27]

What are we to make of this latest story about the Vedic gods? Compared to the one we studied before, it boasts a new cast of characters and a new plot, yet one cannot help being struck by an underlying similarity in the central action. If the problem facing the community is different this time, the method used to solve it is almost the same.

The first myth shows the protagonists at daggers drawn, torn by internal rivalries among multiple, mutually hostile factions. Who would be capable of restoring unity to the camp of the gods? No one was up to this task. Therefore they levied, each from his own person, those of their bodies that were dear to them, and they made these into a single mass that became Indra, or the sun. In the second myth, the rampant internal divisions have given way to a confrontation between a lone individual, Prajapati, and all the other members of the group. The hostility that previously plagued the community has not disappeared, but it is now directed at a single target. Everyone shares in the outrage provoked by the scandalous behavior of Prajapati. There is thus no longer any need to find someone capable of restoring unity to the camp of the gods: Prajapati has quite obligingly performed this feat by uniting them against himself. The only problem left is to find someone capable of punishing him. No one is up to the task of smiting the Lord of Creatures. The gods therefore resort to a procedure that is already familiar to us from the first myth. Except that this time, it is not the most precious parts of themselves that they levy, but the most terrifying; and when all the individual contributions are pooled together, it is not the sun god, Indra, who emerges, but the divine executioner, Rudra. Yet we may ask whether this dark god is not the hidden face of the sun.

In the compact of the gods, each partner cedes to the collectivity the bodies he holds dear in the guise of hostages. Now, if any one of them transgresses the pact, the punishment that awaits him is simply that the corporeal separation becomes definitive—the very same separation that, as Malamoud remarks, is already his lot as long as he remains faithful to the alliance.[28] So, in a sense, even in the first myth, the violence that awaits the transgressor is already present at the origin in virtual form.

But I think this first myth cries out to be read in conjunction with the second. Even though the story of Rudra is on the surface a quite distinct myth, and one that Malamoud discusses in a completely different context, it could be read as a gloss on the myth of Indra. The dismembering violence that in its virtual form is constitutive of Indra becomes identified with Rudra when it is viewed as actual violence. Our metagod thus has two faces. As the guarantor of the harmony and prosperity of the community, he is the benevolent Indra; as the "sacred executioner,"[29] he turns into the terrifying Rudra. In both cases, the circular mechanism of self-transcendence is the same. It is a mechanism that overcomes divisions through unanimity. Only the "single mass" that was Rudra had the "strength and cruelty necessary to transpierce Prajapati." The metagod is born of unanimity.

I would like to end this chapter as I began it: with the story of a miracle. Once again, it is a story that Olivier Herrenschmidt heard in contemporary India. Three outsiders came to a village at festival time, just as the local people were preparing to make a sacrifice. They grabbed one of the newcomers and placed his head in the gibbet. "*He was alone, they could do anything,*" comments the native informant, starkly summing up the power inherent in the configuration of all against one. It looked as if nothing could stop the foreordained sacrifice from taking place. The victim prepared to meet his fate.

Then, as in Giraudoux's play, something happened at the last minute that changed everything. Suddenly, the intended victim was no longer alone—his two companions appeared and began singing an invocation to two of the best-loved figures in the Hindu pantheon: "Rama, Rama, Sita Rama!" As a result, "the sacrificer was unable to budge his arm. All at once, there were hundreds singing, and the others were only a few dozen." In the end, the human sacrifice did not take place. And from that day forward, the festival has been celebrated without putting anyone to death.[30]

This Indian story ends more happily than Giraudoux's play, suggesting that even in the worst of circumstances, violence is never an unstoppable destiny. The most striking thing about the story is the way the process of mimetic contagion itself turns against the sacrificers. One might speak here of the self-transcendence of self-transcendence. A chance happening, the arrival of the two friends in the nick of time, is enough to nudge the mimetic process in another direction and to send it hurtling toward a different fixed point.

But there is more at work here than mere chance. I think this story highlights a way in which mimetic theory leaves an opening for the positive impact of voluntary human action on the historical process. The opening lies in the importance of unanimity to the all-against-one dynamic of the scapegoat mechanism. This requirement for unanimity magnifies the power of those who break with the sacrificial consensus. It only took two people to speak up—or sing out—and the sacrificer's arm stopped miraculously in midair. Just as unanimity was necessary to fortify the arm of the divine executioner Rudra against Prajapati, so the smallest lapse in unanimity was enough to paralyze the arm of this human sacrificer.

Let me close this chapter by quoting a comment on voluntary human action that comes from Herrenschmidt's Indian informants. Their sacrifices are no longer performed with human victims, they explain, because "nobody would volunteer!"[31]

CHAPTER 5

Madness in the Making

The Madman burst into their midst and pierced them with his gaze. "Whither is God!" he cried. "I shall tell you."
— Friedrich Nietzsche, *The Gay Science*, aphorism 125

Maybe I am the Madman himself reincarnated, the one in the aphorism, of whom no one ever speaks.
— René Girard, "The Founding Murder in the Philosophy of Nietzsche"

René Girard knows where it all began. "All religious rituals spring from the surrogate victim," he writes, "and all the great institutions of mankind, both secular and religious, spring from ritual." Not merely some great institutions, or even most, but all—including, to name but a few, "political power, legal institutions, medicine, the theater, philosophy, and anthropology itself."[1]

Now, such a sweeping hypothesis might strike some as a case of reductionism gone mad. How could one simple notion possibly do justice to the overwhelming variety of religious rituals and other social institutions? More to the point, how could anyone imagine that it could?

Faced with the all-encompassing scope of what he sardonically calls his *idée fixe*, Girard admits that he "sometimes cannot help wondering about it" himself.[2] The last straw comes when he discovers yet another instance of his beloved collective murder in the most unsuspected of places, Nietzsche's aphorism 125. Although the actual title of the aphorism is "The Madman," it is better known by the famous phrase it contains: "God is dead!" Intoning this phrase "is the Pavlovian reflex of modernity," Girard remarks, and yet no one seems to remember the sentences that follow: "God remains dead! And it is we who have killed Him." Stumbling upon this forgotten allusion to collective murder has a dizzying effect on Girard, who inevitably identifies with the Madman who utters them. "I feel as if I were going mad," he complains.[3]

Given this self-confessed pathology, it is perhaps no wonder that one of the few specialists to have truly grasped Girard's hypothesis and adapted it to his own field is a man with extensive professional experience in dealing with the mad: Doctor Henri Grivois, the French psychiatrist. It "is not Girard who helped me understand my patients," Grivois explains, "but the patients who enlightened me about Girard's work."[4] We shall examine Grivois's theory of psychosis in a moment. First, however, it is important to clarify the status of the surrogate victim or scapegoat hypothesis and to explain why, in reality, the diagnosis of rampant reductionism misses the mark.

The key is to distinguish between the stark unicity of the hypothesis and the immeasurable diversity that it permits. Girard does not see surrogate victims everywhere, and he does not claim that all institutions are the same. Rather than glossing over differences in reductionist fashion, he sets out to determine how differences can emerge where before there were none. What he proposes is thus a morphogenetic theory of the origins of human culture.[5] This theory does not reduce all institutions to instances of scapegoating; instead, it presents the surrogate victim mechanism as capable of generating the real diversity of cultural forms. "It is impossible . . . to object to the hypothesis on the grounds that primitive institutions are too numerous and too different to be forced into a single mold," writes Girard. "There is no mold at all, but we fail to realize that fact unless we grasp the element of *interpretation* . . . that intervenes between the de facto reconciliation of unanimous victimage and the religious imperatives that stem from it."[6]

Cultural diversity begins with the divergent lines of interpretation to which the astounding reconciliation achieved by the founding murder lends itself: "The inability of religious thought to understand correctly the violent mechanism of its own genesis gives rise to countless interpretations that can all be different from each other because they are all erroneous; these interpretations are the rituals and myths of all human societies the world over."[7] To call religious interpretations "erroneous" is to grant that they are not entirely without foundation. In this sense, Girard takes ritual and mythology far more seriously than do those who hail them as pure products of the unbridled imagination. For Girard, they are misguided attempts to interpret a real event. "It is from such deluded interpretation that the ever-changing forms of sacrificial re-enactment (ritual) and communal recollection (mythology) are generated," Girard emphasizes, "not from the event itself."[8] The delusions are always different; the event is always the same.

The delusions are always different; the event is always the same: this is the conclusion Henri Grivois has reached concerning the nature of the psychotic break. As the head of the psychiatric emergency service at the Hôtel-Dieu general hospital in Paris, Grivois had the opportunity to observe and question patients suffering their first mental breakdown, patients not yet classified according to the traditional nosography and dispatched into a standard institutional framework. Seeking to discover if such patients had anything in common before they entered into one or another chronic form of mental illness, he drew them out when communication was possible and listened attentively to their accounts of what was happening to them. He found that every patient had experienced the same type of event, an event whose unchanging structure can be characterized by three points:

- a feeling of being at the center of the totality of others: *unanimity*
- surprise and astonishment at occupying this position all alone: *absolute singularity*
- initial inability to attribute a meaning to this situation: *Why?*

It is the urgent need to understand "why" that leads those grappling with what Grivois calls "nascent psychosis" (*psychose naissante*) to embark on the path of delusional constructions. In their desperate attempts to understand their astounding situation, patients spin out equally astounding interpretations. These interpretations diverge in certain characteristic directions that depend in part on the patient's individual personality, thus furnishing elements the psychiatrist may seize upon in order to formulate a diagnosis. So it is that the initial "unstable situation issues in a series of bifurcations: every possible point of exit from nascent psychosis is also a point of entry into psychosis in the traditional sense of the word."[9]

As Grivois comments, "the isomorphism of the central crisis in nascent psychosis and of the sacrificial crisis of Girardian anthropology cannot be in doubt."[10] The comparison between the two is all the more compelling insofar as psychotics often resort to religious language or imagery in their efforts to come to grips with a situation that has no parallel in normal experience. Moreover, whether or not they employ an explicitly religious terminology, the delusional interpretations elaborated by psychotics are mythological in the sense that they are typically built upon the choice of a scapegoat, the question "why?" being easily transformed into "who?" Who is responsible for the patient's predicament: a next-door neighbor, the CIA, aliens from another planet? Or perhaps the patient bears full responsibility for committing some mysterious sin that brought on the situation? In the worst cases, such divergent scapegoating interpretations culminate in actions that are properly sacrificial: murder or suicide.

Grivois understands psychotic delusions in the same way that Girard understands religious delusions: not as pure products of a fevered imagination, but as erroneous interpretations of a real event. But what is the correct interpretation of the event in the case of the psychotic crisis? Here there is a danger of carrying the comparison with the sacrificial crisis too far. Even when a murderous or suicidal psychotic commits a sacrificial act, the psychotic is not the victim of collective violence. The unanimity that characterizes the event described by Grivois as common to all nascent psychoses is not—at least not at first—the sacrificial unanimity of all-against-one. The more neutral formula of "unanimity minus one" better sums up the situation of the psychotic, who finds himself in what Grivois defines as a "symmetrical relationship with the totality of human beings."[11] The isomorphism of the psychotic crisis and the sacrificial crisis is limited to this symmetrical relationship between one member of the community and everybody else. It all begins with a lone individual facing the crowd.

In his quest for origins, Girard looks behind the seemingly boundless diversity of social institutions, and what he sees every time is the undifferentiated crowd. His real theme is the formation of the social bond, and for him this means the problem of how to organize the crowd. This was also Sigmund Freud's problem in *Group Psychology and the Analysis of the Ego*. In this book Freud undertakes to study the crowd, but his analysis is not centered on the spontaneous, ephemeral gatherings that interested earlier crowd theorists such as Gustave Le Bon and Gabriel Tarde, but rather on the church, the army, and other examples of what he calls "artificially" constructed crowds, crowds organized around a leader. In this sense Freud's vision of the crowd is poles apart from the anarchy of Girard's sacrificial crisis. And yet, as Jean-Pierre Dupuy emphasizes, Freud turns at a crucial moment to the "disorganized" crowd in order to reach what he calls "the *paradoxical* position that this group mind does away with itself in one of its most striking manifestations."[12] For, as Freud is forced to admit, the crowd that most manifests its identity as a crowd is not the organized group, it is the panicked mob.

Dupuy homes in on the paradoxical case of the panicked mob as a matter of methodological principle: "If the social bond is invisible, it is when it unravels that one has the best chance of perceiving its effects, via the void left behind, as it were."[13] Grivois's lesson is that the unraveling of the mind in madness is fundamentally an unraveling of the social bond. From the solitary madman to the madding crowd, it is always a question of a radical fracture in the bond that links each individual to the others as a whole. Examining what happens when a social group breaks apart into a panicked mob may help us better understand what happens when an individual breaks away from a social group in nascent psychosis.

A crowd that is seized by panic has lost, in Jean-Pierre Dupuy's terminology, its "operator of totalization." For Freud, the operator in question can only be the leader, that narcissistic individual who, by attracting to himself the love of all the others, makes it possible for them to transcend their own narcissism. The love of everyone for the leader gives rise to an "identification" among all those who share this same libidinal object, and it is this identification that in turn founds the "emotional contagion" so characteristic of crowds. The "affective charge of the individuals becomes intensified," Freud tells us, "by mutual interaction. Something is unmistakably at work in the nature of a compulsion to do the same as the others, to remain in harmony with the many."[14]

The difficulty arises when it comes time to explain how all the members of the crowd are able to panic "in harmony," each the same as the others.

For, as Freud acknowledges, the emotional contagion can attain "enormous proportions" when a crowd panics at the loss of its leader, even though this loss necessarily entails the disappearance of the ties of identification among the members of the crowd: "the mutual ties . . . disappear, as a rule, at the same time as the tie with their leader," Freud observes.[15]

In order to resolve this paradox that Freud does no more than report, Dupuy deconstructs in Girardian fashion the supposed narcissism of the leader. Freud compares the leader to Nietzsche's superman. Such a leader has no need to love anyone, Freud insists. He is endowed with the nature of a master; his narcissism is absolute.[16] In other words, the leader in no way needs the crowd, it is the crowd that needs the leader. Without a leader, the crowd is lost. Whereas, without a crowd . . .

Now that one thinks of it, has anybody ever heard of a leader without a crowd?

We shall come back to the idea of a "leader without a crowd." First we must finish examining Dupuy's critique of Freud. What Dupuy does is to subsume the leader's supposed narcissism under the rubric of Girardian "pseudo-narcissism." The apparent self-sufficiency of the leader then stands revealed as an illusion that rests, in circular fashion, on the admiration that it inspires in others: "Isn't it . . . because [the leader] has *already* conquered them that he gives the impression of being able to do without them?"[17] An illusory impression, one understands, since the leader is no exception to the rule according to which "one can only love oneself to the extent that others love you."[18]

The love of Narcissus for himself is but the echo of Echo's love for him. It is Echo who holds out his image to him in a flattering mirror: Echo, the indispensable model who allows him to take himself as object. In the same way, it is the crowd that allows the leader to take himself as object; the narcissism he displays is the echo of the cheers of the crowd. The latter thus provides a model for the leader's narcissistic love—just as the leader, in taking himself as object, provides a model for the crowd's love for him. Between the crowd and its leader, there is an "affective charge" that "becomes intensified by mutual interaction." Far from being the natural and absolute endowment that Freud saw, therefore, the leader's apparent narcissism is the result of a tangled loop: the "process by which the crowd-system closes upon itself."[19] The totalization of the crowd is no longer the work of an external operator, the leader; it is rather the leader who emerges from a process of "self-exteriorization" on the part of the crowd. The leader is actually an endogenous representative of the collectivity.

We may compare the leader of the crowd with Indra, the king of the gods in the Vedic myth analyzed previously. Like the solar divinity Indra, Freud's leader is a radiant figure drawing everyone else into his orbit. Just as the sun burns with its own energy, Freud conceives of the leader as wholly self-sufficient. But we saw that the solar metaphor is misleading. The Vedic myth, less dazzled by the leader's brilliance than Freud, likens Indra to a sun that did not burn at the origin. It is only the energy derived from all the other individuals that allows Indra to shine so brightly. Here the Vedic myth proves its superior perspicacity. It deconstructs the apparent autonomy of the leader, revealing him to be no more than an embodiment of the collectivity.

Now, what happens when panic seizes a crowd that has lost its leader? Dupuy suggests that "there emerges in his stead another representative of the collectivity," equally endogenous and equally transcendent: "it is none other than the collective movement itself, which becomes detached, distances itself and takes on an *autonomy* in relation to individual movements, without ever ceasing, for all that, to be the simple composition of individual actions and reactions."[20] Panic, the contagious phenomenon par excellence, does not require the members of the crowd to be tied to one another by an external mediator; they let themselves be guided in their individual movements by the general movement. It is the collectivity as a whole that constitutes itself as mediator by a process of self-exteriorization, or self-transcendence, and the individuals that compose it are swept up in the turbulence.

Behind the word "turbulence" one finds the Latin term that designates a crowd in effervescence. Freud sought to analyze the crowd with the help of a theory of instincts modeled on classical hydrodynamics. More recently, turbulence as a hydrodynamic structure has become an object of study for the science of chaos. Dupuy's crowd theory goes back to the origins of "turbulence" in order to show how mass psychology might become in its turn "a branch of the physics of disordered systems."[21] If we now return to individual psychology and go back to the origins of modern French psychiatry, we shall encounter without delay a problematic that is strangely familiar.

Confronting us at the outset is the apparent narcissism, the self-sufficiency in the face of the masses, of a singular individual: the madman.

"What indeed is the problem posed by the madman," ask Marcel Gauchet and Gladys Swain in their authoritative work on the institution of the asylum,[22] "if not that of a human being shut up in the incoercible solitude of a belief that is his alone, and who must therefore be torn from the compelling egoism of his daydreams and brought back into the midst of the community of minds."[23] The determination to reintegrate the mad into the community—a determination born of the democratic revolution, but pushed to the point of totalitarian delusion—would take as its instrument the asylum, an institutional system meant to bring the patient out of "the egoism of his point of view" and make him think of himself "from the point of view of that impersonal, anonymous other constituted by the collectivity as a whole."[24]

Here is how one of the founders of French psychiatry, Jean-Étienne Dominique Esquirol, put it in 1838. The ideal regulation of an institution for the insane, he affirmed, "provides motives for obedience that inspire less aversion than the will or caprice of a leader. There is, in a like institution, a movement, an activity, a turbulence, into which each resident enters little by little; the most stubborn, most defiant lypemaniac finds himself unwittingly forced to live outside himself, swept up in the general movement."[25]

To mend the broken bond between the community and the madman, to overcome the egoism of the latter, Esquirol counts on what can only be called the self-exteriority of the collectivity. Self-exteriority versus egoism: that is an opposition we have already encountered. Except that, for Dupuy, it was a question of deconstructing the concept of egoism in theory and not, as for Esquirol, of overcoming its reality in practice. If the egoism of the leader does not possess the reality attributed to it, what about that of the madman?

Here we may return to Grivois's work on nascent psychosis. As we have seen, Grivois found that the initial point that characterizes every psychosis at its birth is the "feeling of being at the center of the totality of others"—which would certainly seem, at first sight, to confirm the idea that the madman is fundamentally egoistic, narcissistic, or, better yet, downright megalomaniacal. However, the two other points that complete the clinical portrait put into question the common assumption of a "return to infantile megalomania." In addition to the feeling of being at the center of everyone else, we saw that an individual in the throes of nascent psychosis also manifests "surprise and astonishment at occupying this position all alone" and an "inability to attribute a meaning to this situation." Now, if this individual were endowed, like Freud's leader, with absolute narcissism, he would quite naturally expect to be at the center of the world and would hardly be amazed to find himself there. The madman's surprise and lack of understanding are, on the contrary, normal reactions in the face of an extraordinary situation. After all, if you suddenly found yourself truly at the center of the world, you, too, would be surprised and would want to know why.

Why, from each person whose path you cross, in the subway or on the street, does there emanate a strange "concernedness" (*concernement*), to employ the suggestive term that Grivois borrows from Jean Starobinski? What does it mean, this "concernedness" regarding you, as ever-present as it is indecipherable? We must try to put ourselves in the shoes of the patients whose experience Grivois conveys through extracts from his clinical notes. "A. says right off that she is at the center of the world. 'It's a pack, of women, men, children, teenagers, old folks.' She doesn't know what the pack's intentions are or else she defines them in extremely varied fashion: hostility, protection?"[26] It is this radical uncertainty that proves so unbearable and explains the "manic" state of a person in the throes of nascent psychosis.

Later, perhaps, the patient will recover a relative calm by fixing on a single interpretation of his new relationship with others—an interpretation that must be commensurable with the extraordinary nature of the situation. "Paul is God incarnate, Raphael acts and thinks like a supercomputer, Margit is the victim designated by everyone, Arnaud is a scientific messiah, Philippe has been delegated by God to manage the world."[27] But, as we saw earlier, the adoption of such delusional interpretations already signals the end of nascent psychosis and the entry into one of the psychoses catalogued in the official nosography. Depending on the direction in which the patient's interpretation of his experience diverges, the subsequent chronic psychosis will be classified differently. And yet, diverse as these delusions may be, they all reflect their common morphogenesis in a real event.

We still need to clarify the nature of this event. Earlier, we said that the subject finds himself suddenly thrust into a situation of unanimity-minus-one. Why does the experience of this situation give rise so invariably to supernatural interpretations of one kind or another? Why does it produce a feeling of transcendence?

The transcendence in question is perhaps best expressed by Étienne, a patient of Grivois's who exclaimed to everyone he met upon arriving at the hospital, "I am everybody! I am you! And you! And you!"[28] In other words, "I am the incarnation of the collectivity." And that, of course, is Durkheim's definition of divinity. In their own ways, Paul, Margit, Arnaud, and Raphael echo Étienne when they claim to be God incarnate or a universal victim, a scientific messiah or a supercomputer. The same equivalence between being a god, ruler, or savior and being anybody and everybody is likewise apparent in Gilles Deleuze and Félix Guattari's characterization of the feeling inspired by schizophrenic delirium: "I become God, I become woman, I was Joan of Arc, and I am Heliogabale, and the Great Mogul, a Chinese, an Indian, a Templar, I was my father and I was my son. And all criminals."[29] This haphazard enumeration identifies divinity with a breakdown of basic cultural, sexual, and kinship distinctions reminiscent of Girard's sacrificial crisis. In the case of madness, however, it is associated not with the breakdown of society but with the breakdown of an individual's link to society.

The latter type of breakdown—a "mental" breakdown—is a personal catastrophe that may occur for many reasons that science has yet to understand fully. Even if it turns out that these reasons include a cognitive or perceptual dysfunction of organic origin, such a rupture in normal functioning is bound to provoke a rupture in the subject's relations with others. And once it occurs, the rupture of the normal, multiple, differentiated bond, the bond to others in their individuality, gives rise to a unique and undifferentiated bond to others in their totality: anybody and everybody. For, whatever happens, it is impossible for a social being to have no relation at all with others— "Does not an imponderable concernedness emerge from two persons as soon as their eyes meet?" remarks Grivois[30]—and a bond with the human race as a whole is all that remains in the absence of other bonds.

Now, as soon as one finds oneself plunged into a relationship with the entire rest of the human race, one cannot help displaying what Gauchet and Swain rightly define as the "minimal feature of subjective pathology": namely, the conviction that one is in some way unique, one of a kind, a category unto oneself.[31] This conviction, which seems intrinsically egotistical, could thus be merely the logical consequence of the relational rupture that marks the entry into psychosis. It is the conviction of being radically alone, of facing the rest of the human race as one big undifferentiated crowd.

This is how we may understand the claim that psychotic delusions are rooted in the experience of a real event. "The crowd is real," Grivois declares.

"It takes on and gives to everything monstrous dimensions, but at the same time it maintains the subject in an intense social life."[32] Durkheim, the pre-eminent theorist of "collective effervescence," will help us understand these words. He observes that a "very intense social life always does to the organism, as to the individual consciousness, a sort of violence that disturbs its normal functioning." Why, then, should we be surprised by the delusional interpretations produced by someone experiencing such intense interactions with others? Why, given that, once more according to Durkheim, "if one terms delirium any state in which the mind adds to what is immediately given by sensory intuition and projects its feelings and its impressions into things, there is perhaps no collective representation that, in a sense, is not delirious"?[33]

The answer is obviously that the madman's representation is not that of the collectivity, and that the interaction in question appears rather as an alienation. But the alienation resides in the fact that the madman participates intensely in a social interaction with partners who, for their part, do not see it in the same light. The person suffering from nascent psychosis manifests quite precisely what Durkheim describes as "the peculiar attitude of a man talking to a crowd":

> His language has a sort of grandiloquence that would be ridiculous in ordinary circumstances; there is something dominating about his gestures; his very thinking is impatient of proportion and easily allows itself to go to every extreme. That is because he feels as if he were overflowing with an abnormal plethora of forces that tend to spread out from him; sometimes he even has the impression that he is dominated by a moral power that transcends him and of which he is but the interpreter.... Now, this exceptional surplus of forces is quite real: it comes from the very group that he is addressing. The feelings that his words arouse come back to him, but swollen, amplified, and they reinforce his own feelings to the same degree.[34]

The madman is the one who adopts this "peculiar attitude" without realizing that he finds himself in "ordinary circumstances." He is the one who speaks as a leader at the head of a crowd when no crowd follows him. In short, if panic is the "crowd without a leader," then the madman is the "leader without a crowd."

At least that is how he is perceived—by the crowd: the real crowd, the one composed of everyone he meets. To be sure, whereas Durkheim specifies that he is depicting an orator who has "succeeded in entering into communion"[35] with the crowd, the crowd is not at all in communion with the madman. The difference between the leader and the madman is comparable to that between Richard Wagner and Nietzsche in Girard's analysis:

> Bayreuth is presented by Nietzsche as Wagner's monstrous effort to organize his own cult. Nietzsche may not be completely wrong, but *Ecce Homo* is exactly the same thing. It is Nietzsche's effort to organize his own cult. . . . The only difference, of course, is that Wagner has real worshippers, whereas Nietzsche has no one but himself. . . . The complete silence around him forces Nietzsche into more and more histrionics, the type of behavior that must be acknowledged as characteristically schizophrenic. . . . The difference between the healthy man and the sick one, at this stage, may be their more or less successful relationship to the crowd.[36]

To borrow Freud's expression, the madman does not succeed in achieving "harmony with the many." But once the madman's histrionics become extreme enough to rouse the crowd out of its silence, a charge will be sparked between the madman and the crowd that is "intensified by mutual interaction." Like Durkheim's orator, who gives the impression of "something dominating" about him while experiencing all the while the "impression that he is dominated," the madman is caught up in a circularity. The more excited he becomes, the more he will excite concern in those around him. And once the intensity of the "concernedness" centered upon him becomes too much for him, he is liable to commit an act that is too much for the community—at which point the gendarmes will arrive to cart him off to Doctor Grivois's mental ward. The tangled loop of the "crowd-system" brings about the expulsion—the "exteriorization"—of its center.

Given the circularity of the process involved, does the expulsion of the madman qualify as another example of "*self*-exteriorization"? It does, but with an important distinction. In the case of the crowd-system centered on the leader, Dupuy describes the latter as a focal point "produced by the crowd even though the crowd imagines itself to be its product."[37] Contrary to Freud's belief, the leader does not possess the self-sufficiency of a Nietzschean superman; the leader's apparent narcissism is the product of the unanimous love the crowd directs at him. Similarly, in the case of Girard's surrogate victim, the unanimous violence the crowd directs at it is what allows the victim to appear as a savior: the victim's expulsion saves the crowd from its own violence. The victim's divinity is thus produced by the crowd even though the crowd imagines it owes its salvation to the victim's divinity.

The leader and the victim are both examples of the "self-exteriorization" of the crowd. The crowd exteriorizes itself in the person of the individual it exalts or expels. The impetus in these two cases comes from the crowd. In the case of the madman, however, the process is reversed. This time the impetus comes from the individual. Initially, the crowd is indifferent; it is the madman himself who, by directing indiscriminate love or violence at the crowd, triggers his own victimization. The madman allows us to witness the crisis of the social bond from the tail end. In fact, it is a case of the tail wagging the dog; the madman's belief that the crowd is polarized against him is what ultimately produces such a polarization of the crowd. This time the "self" in the "self-exteriorization" is the madman: he succeeds in communicating his own alienation to the crowd, alienating it from him. The madman is thus an individual who exteriorizes himself in the "person" of the crowd: the madman's focal point is the crowd as a whole. A paradoxical focal point, to be sure, but one that is not new to us: we have already encountered it in the case of panic. Like the "crowd without a leader," the "leader without a crowd" has the collective movement as its focal point.

Grivois's patients are picked up by the police for creating a public disturbance; they are compelled to seek out the crowd. Nietzsche's Madman is no different; he heads straight for the public square: "Haven't you heard about the Madman who, having lit a lantern under the noonday sun, ran to the marketplace and cried incessantly, 'I seek God! I seek God!'" And he cannot really have been surprised when his outlandish behavior "provoked much laughter."[38] After all, Girard observes, he "provokes his listeners with his strange symbolism of the lantern lit under the noonday sun." But Girard goes on to suggest that the Madman's effort to provoke an antagonistic reaction from the crowd is not merely perverse: "By polarizing the many against him the Madman hopes to arouse the curiosity of the rare individuals liable to comprehend him."[39]

Girard's interest here is in the surrogate victim mechanism, and he is referring to the inability of the "vulgar atheists" in the crowd to comprehend the Madman's revelation of the collective murder of God. But if we have an interest in the mechanism of madness, we may see another meaning. When a madman seeks out the crowd and cries "I seek God," what the vulgar atheists who laugh in disbelief do not comprehend is that, collectively, they are God. Indeed, Grivois's therapeutic technique could be said to rest on the premise that communication with the mad is possible once this fundamental identification has been grasped. Take the case of Étienne, the patient who arrived in Grivois's clinic exclaiming "I am everybody! I am you! And you!" Grivois was able to facilitate contact with him by replying mildly, "Yes, that is why you are God." If the reality behind the experience of transcendence common to nascent psychosis is finding oneself alone in the face of everybody else, the fact that at least one other person—the therapist—joins the patient in recognizing this experience may already suffice, as Grivois suggests, to transform that reality: to break the unanimity of unanimity-minus-one.

Only the mad can see firsthand that momentous phenomenon Girard helps us understand: the origin of divinity in unanimity-minus-one. Is the madman a seer? Part of the modern mystique of madness, its aura of romantic glamour, is doubtless a mere automatic byproduct of the expulsion of the mad from the community: a secondary divinization on the part of those who always side with the victim (however crazy) against the crowd (however justified). We have suggested that the medical confinement of the mad is not an arbitrary playing-out of the scapegoat mechanism: the madman provokes his own expulsion. Moreover, as Gauchet and Swain forcefully remind us, the modern asylum was not meant to remove the mad permanently from the community, but, on the contrary, to remove them from the isolation of their alienation—in Esquirol's words, to bring them back into the "general movement."

As we have also seen, however, there is more to madness than self-expulsion. The confrontation with the community that results in putting the mad away is posterior to what we have called the "real event" at the root of madness: not a communal assault on the individual—all against one—but a rupture of the bond that ties the individual to the community—unanimity minus one. The psychotic may well construct a delusional interpretation of this unanimity as being directed against him, in which case he will easily perceive the collective reaction his behavior subsequently provokes as retrospectively confirming that interpretation. But the fact that he voices a deluded interpretation of an expulsion that he himself provokes must not blind us to the fact that his delusions are rooted in an initial unanimity not of his own doing, the unanimity-minus-one of nascent psychosis.

Again, this unanimity-minus-one is not the same as that of the surrogate victim mechanism. Nonetheless, we have seen that it gives rise in comparable ways to delusions of divinity—delusions that in this case are in the mind of the individual rather than the collectivity. The collectivity knows that the individual is mad. And yet, when a madman "bursts into their midst" and, like Nietzsche's Madman, "pierces them with his gaze,"[40] the crowd also senses dimly that the madman is able to penetrate to a level of reality it cannot see. There is therefore more to the mystique of madness than a modern romanticization of victims. In fact, the attribution of visionary powers to the mad is not a purely modern phenomenon. It is based on the timeless intuition that the madman has witnessed with his own eyes a thing hidden from ordinary mortals, an event they can barely imagine: the birth of the gods.

Girard and the madman both "pierce with their gaze" beyond empirically existing social institutions to the hidden reality of the undifferentiated crowd—but Girard does so as a thought experiment and the madman as one who has directly experienced the disintegration of the social bond. Moreover, a madman has experienced the breaking of the bond from the opposite end. The isomorphism of the individual and social crises is not an identity; the gods of madness are not the gods of violence and the sacred. Yet it is precisely because they are not the same that the delusions of the mad can be said to provide independent confirmation of Girard's thought experiment: they demonstrate in symmetrical fashion the morphogenetic power intrinsic in the schema of unanimity minus one.

CHAPTER 6

No Exit? Madness and the Divided Self

Presence to self . . . supposes that an impalpable fissure has slipped into being. If being is present to itself, it is because it is not wholly itself.

—Jean-Paul Sartre, *Being and Nothingness*

There is a crack in everything.
That's how the light gets in.

—Leonard Cohen, "Anthem"

One day, a man came to see the Japanese psychotherapist Takehisa Kora and announced that he feared going mad. After examining him and finding him quite lucid, Doctor Kora told him his fear was groundless. People who are truly going insane generally do not realize it, the therapist explained. Indeed, the very fact that the patient worried about going crazy proved he was in no danger of actually doing so.

Listening to Doctor Kora's words, the man felt as if a weight had been lifted from his shoulders. He left the therapist's office fully reassured. Barely two weeks later, though, the same patient was back again. "I'm not so anxious any more about going crazy," he said. "So I wonder if I'm not in danger now of *really* going crazy."[1]

Doctor Kora's patient was caught in the tangled loop of a double bind or catch-22. If he worried about going mad, it was a sign he shouldn't worry. But if he stopped worrying, then he had reason to worry again. This catch-22 kept the patient from recovering his serenity. He remained afraid of going mad even though he wasn't.

Thankfully, going crazy is not so easy to do. On the other hand, it is true that a man or woman who does go crazy may well have been sane before. How can a once-sane individual fall prey to psychotic delusions? That was the question explored in the last chapter. Having tried to shed light on the entry into madness, I now take up the plight of the chronically insane and ask why it is so hard to make an exit from madness.

Thinking properly about madness requires confronting the existential dilemmas faced by the mad. Mad individuals wishing to escape their condition may find themselves caught in a double bind—a catch-22 not unlike that of Doctor Kora's patient but one that, this time, stands in the way of recovering sanity. It is a treacherous loop identified by Douglas Hofstadter in a brief but suggestive passage of *Gödel, Escher, Bach.* How can you figure out whether you are sane or not, he asks, "given that you have only your own logic to judge itself? I don't see any answer."[2]

The considerations that follow were originally presented at a Stanford University conference on the paradoxes of self-deception where leading analytic philosophers including Alfred Mele and the late Donald Davidson defended their respective positions. The question posed by self-deception is whether the beliefs in mutually exclusive propositions are themselves mutually exclusive. Can one believe something and, at the same time, believe the opposite? Donald Davidson and Alfred Mele have championed opposing points of view on this question.

For Davidson, self-deception requires the simultaneous presence of contradictory beliefs by definition. A self-deceived person is one whose belief in a proposition is motivated by a belief in the opposite proposition, or at least by the thought that one ought rationally to believe the opposite, so that "the state that motivates self-deception and the state it produces coexist."[3] And the paradox of simultaneous adhesion to incompatible beliefs is resolved by positing a partitioning of the mind that keeps the opposed beliefs apart.[4]

Mele argues, on the contrary, that the hypothesis of mental partitioning may be avoided.[5] He sets out to resolve the paradox by showing that in many cases of what ordinary people mean by "self-deception," it is possible to trace how motivation has influenced belief without there ever being a need to suppose that the self-deceived person "simultaneously holds beliefs whose propositional contents are mutually contradictory."[6] No coexistence of incompatible beliefs, no partitioning of the mind.

For my part, I believe Davidson is right: self-deception involves the simultaneous presence of contradictory beliefs. I also believe Mele is right: self-deception may exist without mental partitioning. My task, then, will be to show that these two propositions are not mutually exclusive. While I will devote particular attention to the problem of madness, my aim is also to demonstrate an approach to self-division that I hope may have more general relevance.

Self-Division in Madness

After analyzing a number of garden-variety instances of self-deception that do not involve simultaneous presence of contradictory beliefs, Mele concludes his Stanford paper by noting that counterexamples might be found in the literature on multiple personality—but he implies that those would be the exceptions that prove the rule: they would involve not self-deception but deception between multiple selves.[7]

Rather than addressing anything so esoteric as multiple personality disorders, I am going to talk about your average, run-of-the-mill lunatics—the sort of individuals who believe they are Jesus Christ, or Napoleon, or the victims of a conspiracy orchestrated by Freemasons from Mars. Now, it is certainly plausible that such manifestly deluded beliefs entail some form of self-deception. After all, even if the individuals in question tell us that their thoughts are electronically implanted into their heads by the CIA, we don't believe that. We consider their thoughts to be internally generated. And, no matter how much weight we might wish to attribute to genetic predisposition in the etiology of mental illness—with genetics filling in for the CIA—it seems unlikely that there could be a specific part of the brain hardwired to believe in Freemasons from Mars, although I suppose an especially determined believer in the modularity of mind might disagree.

It would seem, then, that psychotic delusions may involve an extreme form of self-deception. So extreme, in fact, that one could argue that they constitute a particularly good test case for the partitioning hypothesis. For if mental partitioning is not necessary to allow an otherwise lucid man to maintain in the face of all evidence that he is Napoleon, why should it be needed to permit a woman to embrace the much less intrinsically improbable belief that her husband is not cheating on her? And, indeed, it is perhaps because madness seems to involve extreme self-deception that it has traditionally been associated with some notion of mental division. The idea of division or "splitting" is present, of course, in the prefix "schizo-". The phrase "divided self" also figures in the title of a well-known book by the antipsychiatrist R. D. Laing. However, I will take as my starting point not contemporary antipsychiatrists but the founders of modern French institutional psychiatry.

The idea of a divided self is in fact central to what the philosopher Marcel Gauchet and the late psychiatrist Gladys Swain identify, in *La pratique de l'esprit humain*, as the emancipatory humanist impulse responsible for the birth of modern French psychiatry at the dawn of the nineteenth century.[8] The liberatory thrust of the psychiatric movement they analyze is symbolized by the celebrated story of Doctor Philippe Pinel delivering the inmates of an asylum from their chains—a story all the more significant for being, as Swain has documented, perfectly apocryphal.[9] If this gesture is ascribed to Pinel, it is as a tribute to his role in introducing the so-called "moral treatment" of the mentally ill in France.

The quest for a "moral" or "psychological" treatment of the insane is fundamentally democratic, Gauchet and Swain argue, in that it is based on the recognition that even these archetypal outcasts are fellow human subjects; it is founded on the premise that the mad are not so radically Other that they cannot be reached through communication. What was revolutionary in Pinel's 1801 treatise on "mental alienation" was, Swain writes, its "critique of the idea of complete madness. Mental alienation is never total: the alienated individual always maintains a distance from his alienation." Thus, far from being an opaque object upon which one must act from without, the patient becomes a "torn subjectivity with which a therapeutic exchange is possible."[10] In other words, the mad are not irredeemably mad because they are not totally so; the therapist's hope of communicating with the patient must rest on the possibility of appealing to a healthy component of the diseased self, and hence on the existence of a "*split [clivage]* in the alienated subjectivity."[11]

The alienated display a distance from their own alienation: any Hegelian resonance one may detect in this notion is more than coincidental. In fact, Swain quotes Hegel himself, who credits Pinel with having "discovered that residue of reason in the alienated and in maniacs, having discovered it as containing the principle of their cure, and having directed their treatment according to this principle."[12] Swain emphasizes the extent to which Hegel's reading of Pinel, too often forgotten, foreshadows Freud's own embrace of the notion of "psychic splitting"; in the *Outline of Psychoanalysis*, Freud writes that the "problem of psychosis would be simple and clear if the ego detached itself totally from reality, but that is something that happens rarely, perhaps even never. Even in the case of states as far removed from the reality of the external world as are the confusional hallucinatory states (amentia), the sick, once cured, declare that in a remote corner of their mind, as they put it, a normal person lay in hiding, letting the whole morbid phantasmagoria unfold before him like a disinterested observer."[13]

Here we find ourselves at the heart of the question of mental partitioning in madness. What strikes me about this passage from Freud is that, while it certainly suggests the existence of a boundary within the mind, the image it conjures up seems to be a reversal of the usual one in which the irrational unconscious is walled off and hidden from the rational self. In these extreme psychoses where the irrational has taken over, marginalizing the rational self, it is the other way around: the rational self is hidden, or walled off, from the irrational. This in itself means little insofar as the irrational is in either case impervious to the rational. What is new this time is that the rational self seems to peer out from its hiding place behind the wall and spy on the madness on the other side. It may be helpless to intervene, but it is not unaware of what is going on, even though this awareness will only be expressed later, after the patient is cured.

This passage from Freud himself would thus seem already to suggest that the boundary is less than hermetic. But I will later cite evidence that mental patients are occasionally able to give overt expression to their internal division even before a cure is effected, or at least during an intermediate stage of the cure. As we shall see, however, these expressions necessarily take a paradoxical form. And I will argue that this paradoxical form may even help explain how it is that the coexistence of incompatible beliefs is able to subsist despite the rationality of the mad.

For the most deluded lunatic can be quite rational. There is no shortage of method in madness. I spoke earlier of an "otherwise lucid" man who maintains that he is Napoleon. The madness is in the premise and not necessarily in the way the premise is defended. It is clearly possible to marshal rational argument on behalf of the most delusory premise. Proof of this can be found, if any is needed, in the curious nineteenth-century satire *Historic Doubts Relative to Napoleon Bonaparte*. The author, Richard Whately, devotes a long pamphlet to demonstrating, through careful argument, not that he is Napoleon, but that nobody ever was Napoleon—that in fact the belief in Napoleon is a historically produced delusion: a myth. And it is interesting to note that the point of the satire was to defend the author's real religious faith from the attacks of skeptical authors who used similar methods in their attempts to prove such religious beliefs delusory.[14]

Certainly there are schizophrenics who display apparently disordered and incoherent thinking, but this is typical only at the onset of the illness, when patients are overwhelmed by the enormity of the experience they are going through. It will be helpful to refer here to a distinction Gordon Claridge makes in *Origins of Mental Illness*: "schizophrenia really consists of two elements: temporary changes in dynamic brain processes, such as arousal, which help to precipitate and drive the person into a psychotic state; and delusional thoughts and ideas which form the permanent or relatively permanent bedrock of the schizophrenic condition."[15] Once schizophrenics get past that initial stage of temporary changes in brain processes, many of them find it possible to account for their experience in relatively ordered fashion, erecting elaborate theoretical edifices on the bedrock of delusional thoughts and ideas.

With these schizophrenics, then, it is possible to reason. Indeed, their deployment of rational argument may make it tempting for others to try to reason with them in order to bring them to see the error of their delusions. But, as one can imagine, reasoning with a patient in this way hardly proves to be a successful therapeutic technique. The problem could be the role of motivation in the patient's cognition, to borrow the language used by analytic philosophers. Pinel's disciple Esquirol wrote his thesis on "the passions considered as causes, symptoms, and means of curing mental alienation." In this work, published in 1805, Esquirol writes that critics of the "moral treatment" of mental patients have misunderstood what it is about: "we have never claimed to cure them by arguing with them; that claim would be refuted by everyday experience: do the passions give way to reasoning? Are not alienation, and all its varieties, passions carried to the extreme? To treat them with dialectical formulas and syllogisms would be to show ignorance of the workings of the passions and of the clinical history of mental alienation." In fact, far from being freed of his beliefs, the patient will "adhere to them all the more, the more one strives to dissuade him."[16] And Gladys Swain tells us that all "the authors participating in the new movement concurred on this point: it is as absurd as it is vain—not to say disastrous—to attack the delusional certitude head-on. . . . There is therefore no choice but to 'deal gently with [the patient's] sensitivities.'"[17]

The question may arise at this point as to whether the patient doth protest too much. One could ask if such impassioned defense of delusion is not a manifestation of psychologically motivated resistance to the truth. On the one hand, the mad are capable of "listening to reason" in the sense that they can follow rational argument, but, on the other hand, their madness is impervious to reason inasmuch as no amount of rational argument will win them over. If, indeed, a reasoned attack on the deluded beliefs actually provokes a patient to cling to them all the more strongly, one might surmise that the patient is resisting recognizing something as true out of a belief, or at least a nagging suspicion, that it is true. This resistance would then qualify as self-deception—or, in Sartrean terms, "bad faith."

I will not try to settle the question of whether such a patient's apparent resistance actually does manifest bad faith. Indeed, I propose for the time being to set the question of madness aside entirely and to review Jean-Paul Sartre's analysis of bad faith as a general phenomenon affecting ordinary people. Sartre's demonstration that contradictory beliefs can coexist in the absence of mental partitioning is premised on a type of self-division quite different from that posited by Freud or Davidson. I will argue that this paradoxical type of self-division, which Sartre identifies as endemic to sane minds, is formally related to the type that Gregory Bateson associates with schizophrenia. In the concluding section, I will return to the question of what keeps the mad from being cured. The hypothesis I will present is that even in the absence of bad-faith resistance, the mad may find themselves divided from sanity by a logic formally similar to that of Sartrean bad faith.

Self-Division in Sanity

Sartre's treatment of bad faith is distinguished by his insistence on the inner translucency of the mind, which leads him to reject the Freudian view of resistance. According to Freud, resistance is a phenomenon that manifests itself in the course of psychoanalytic treatment at the very moment the analyst approaches the truth. The essence of Sartre's criticism of Freud is that resistance to knowledge necessarily implies awareness of what is being resisted and hence the absence of an impermeable boundary between the contradictory beliefs. Whereas Freudian resistance rests on a division of the mind into consciousness and the unconscious, Sartre's version of self-deception as bad faith emphasizes "the unity of a *single* consciousness": "I must know in my capacity as deceiver the truth which is hidden from me in my capacity as the one deceived. Better yet I must know the truth very exactly *in order* to conceal it more carefully—and this not at two different moments, which at a pinch would allow us to re-establish a semblance of duality—but in the unitary structure of a single project."[18]

To avoid the paradoxical unity inherent in the fact of deceiving oneself, psychoanalysis "replaces the duality of the deceiver and the deceived . . . by that of the 'id' and the 'ego.'" By introducing this distinction, Sartre observes, "Freud has cut the psychic whole into two. I *am* the ego but I *am not* the *id*." I am thus encouraged to view part of myself as if it were an external reality, a thing existing "*in itself*" the way a table does.[19] With this argument, Sartre in effect accuses psychoanalysis itself of being a sophisticated instrument of bad faith, since for Sartre a typical ploy of bad faith is precisely to try to deny one's freedom by constituting oneself as an inert reality beyond one's own reach. And yet, Sartre notes, despite the "materialistic mythology of psychoanalysis," despite "all the metaphors representing the repression as the impact of blind forces," Freud cannot get around the fact that there can be no repression without an awareness of what is to be repressed—without an awareness of it "*as to be repressed*."[20]

As a result, Freud finds himself in a bind. On the one hand, he does not want to attribute this self-aware activity of repression to the conscious ego, but, on the other hand, he cannot ascribe it to the unconscious complex itself either, for the "complex as such is rather the collaborator of the psychoanalyst since"—by smuggling clues past the repression—"it aims at expressing itself in clear consciousness."[21] Freud's solution is to assign the responsibility for repression to a hypothetical censor, "conceived," Sartre remarks sardonically, "as a line of demarcation with customs, passport division, currency control, *etc.*"[22] The "reflexive idea of hiding something from oneself" necessarily implies a "double activity" that tends both "to maintain and locate the thing to be concealed" and "to repress and disguise it," Sartre concludes. "By separating consciousness from the unconscious by means of the censor, psychoanalysis . . . has merely localized this double activity of repulsion and attraction on the level of the censor." And what is this censor if not a "hypostasized and 'reified'" version of bad faith?[23] By setting up the censor as a third party, psychoanalysis cuts the Gordian knot of *self*-deception: I am not deceived by myself at all, but by the censor who keeps me from seeing the unconscious drive. But to say that the unconscious drive is repressed by an agent of repression called the "censor" amounts to no more than putting a name on the phenomenon to be explained. The end result, Sartre comments, is "a mere verbal terminology."[24]

Writing after the first publication of the present text, a defender of psychoanalysis, Simon Boag, has responded to the argument outlined here by acknowledging that the censor, conceived "as a separate, superior agency, is implausible and should be rejected." However, Boag shows that Freud also provides "a clear alternative account of repression" based on a picture of the mind as an "economy of competing motives." In this account, "repression involves a conflict between motivational systems and not between an impulse and a superior, transcendental censor."[25] Indeed, in his *Introductory Lectures on Psycho-Analysis*, Freud himself warns against taking the idea of a censor "too anthropomorphically" and picturing it as "a severe little manikin or a spirit living in a closet in the brain" from which it carries out its censorial duties. "For the time being," Freud writes, "it is nothing more than a serviceable term for describing a dynamic relation."[26] Yet, despite this caveat, Freud sometimes cannot seem to help conjuring up a transcendent figure charged with the censorship function; he wavers back and forth between alternative conceptions without ever reconciling them. "Freud appears to hold two seemingly contrary pictures of the mind," Boag remarks, "one explicable in terms of mechanistic operations"—the "impact of blind forces" to which

Sartre alludes—and "the other in terms of agency and 'persons.'"[27] How can Freud maintain two apparently incompatible beliefs about the operation of repression? Is he guilty of self-deception?

As Freud himself recognizes, the censor cannot be an all-seeing homunculus or "spirit" acting from a hidden command post within the brain. Such an image of a separate, transcendent entity is clearly mythical. But, as I argued earlier in this book, a mythical transcendent figure may conceal something real—something that emerges as a system effect from the interaction of lower-order entities. We have seen how the interaction of the Vedic gods gives rise to the "metagod" Indra. The two strands in Freud's thinking about repression described by Simon Boag may be reconciled if we understand the transcendent censor as the avatar of a comparable metalevel entity. In Freud's alternative account of repression, what looks like censorship is simply the outcome of a "dynamic relation" between conflicting affective impulses. "As such," Boag emphasizes, "the protagonists of the conflict are *qualitatively* similar" to one another—none truly occupies a superior or transcendent position.[28] But I would add that, by the same token, no individual protagonist is qualitatively similar to the overall equilibrium that emerges from the "economy of competing motives." It is to capture the metalevel status of this emergent equilibrium or "fixed point" that Freud resorts to the metaphor of the censor.

As an anthropomorphic embodiment of the mechanism through which an equilibrium emerges from the "economy of competing motives," the Freudian censor plays a role in psychoanalytic theory comparable to that of the Walrasian auctioneer in neoclassical economics. The French mathematical economist Léon Walras used the functioning of an auction house as a metaphor for the process through which equilibrium prices emerge in a market economy. As Jean-Pierre Dupuy emphasizes, this was no more than a "manner of speaking" for Walras, "a figurative way of picturing how markets work: *as if* they resembled an auction house. Not for a moment did he believe that this primitive thought experiment described how markets *actually* work."[29] Likewise, it seems clear that Freud never intended the metaphor of the censor to be taken literally. Unfortunately, it is a misleading metaphor insofar as it confuses an endogenous or internally generated fixed point with an exogenous one, thus producing the transcendent figure so effectively ridiculed by Sartre. Yet Freudian repression may appear less implausible if we see it as the result of a spontaneous process of *self*-transcendence.

Nevertheless, Sartre's critique of the censor has a broader relevance. Any theory of mental partitioning in self-deception must reckon with it. Sartre's fundamental point is that one cannot limit the scope of consciousness by positing the existence of a wall inside the mind without also positing the existence of an independent consciousness to mind the wall.[30] But if the wall cannot be effective without a homunculus to man Checkpoint Charlie, we will have traded in the paradoxical unity of self-deception for a merely implausible duality. Of course, the paradoxical unity will remain equally implausible until it has been better elucidated. It is clearly not enough to label it paradoxical and to leave it at that. The question remains: How is bad faith possible?

For his part, Sartre counters with an unexpected question: How is sincerity possible? Examining sincerity is an indirect route to understanding bad faith. If bad faith is hopelessly paradoxical, presumably its antithesis, sincerity, should be unproblematic. Sartre proceeds to demonstrate that this is far from being the case. Absolute sincerity with regard to oneself is, he argues, an impossible ideal. The "maxim 'one must be what one is' . . . posits not merely an ideal of knowing but an ideal of *being*; it proposes for us an absolute equivalence of being with itself. . . . In this sense it is necessary that we *make ourselves* what we are."[31] But that "supposes that I am not originally what I am." Rather, "I can *become* sincere; this is what my duty and my effort to achieve sincerity imply." Yet if I am not already what I am to begin with, no amount of effort will succeed in making me what I am, and "all movement toward being in itself or 'being what one is'" must be impossible. Moreover, "this impossibility is not hidden from consciousness; on the contrary, it is the very stuff of consciousness; it is the embarrassing constraint which we constantly experience; it is our very incapacity to recognize ourselves, to constitute ourselves as being what we are."[32]

This "embarrassing constraint" is intrinsic to consciousness. By consciously endeavoring to identify what we are, as one would identify a mere thing, an external object, we cannot avoid constituting ourselves as external to ourselves—and thus as *not* what we are.[33] In attempting to see ourselves for what we are, to observe ourselves, we inevitably find that the self doing the observing is not the self that is observed: "as soon as we posit ourselves as a certain being . . . then by that very positing we surpass this being."[34] Indeed, if we do not like what we are, we can even resort to sincerity as a kind of dodge

to escape being what we are: "Who can not see that the sincere man constitutes himself as a thing in order to escape the condition of a thing by the
same act of sincerity?" For example, the "man who confesses that he is evil
has exchanged his disturbing 'freedom for evil' for an inanimate character of
evil; he *is* evil. . . . But by the same stroke, he escapes from that *thing*, since
it is he who contemplates it." In performing the meritorious act of sincerely
confessing himself to be evil, he "is not the evil man as he is evil but as he is
beyond his evilness." Hence the adage "A sin confessed is half pardoned."[35]

From the foregoing considerations, Sartre is able to conclude, not only
that sincerity is as paradoxical as bad faith, but that "the essential structure
of sincerity does not differ from that of bad faith since the sincere man
constitutes himself as what he is *in order not to be it*."[36] The ideal of sincerity—to be what I am—turns out to be "a task impossible to achieve, of which
the very meaning is in contradiction with the structure of my consciousness." Whether in good faith or bad faith, I cannot get around the fact that
"*consciousness is not what it is*."[37] If consciousness could be what it is, if I as
a conscious being could be what I am, then bad faith would be not only
paradoxical, but "forever impossible."[38] But the analysis of sincerity shows the
impossibility of consciously being what I am—and therefore the possibility
of consciously failing to be what I am: "Bad faith is possible only because
sincerity is conscious of missing its goal inevitably, due to its very nature."[39]

"How can we believe by bad faith in the concepts which we forge
expressly to persuade ourselves?" Sartre asks. In other words, how is it possible to deceive ourselves by making ourselves believe the opposite of what we
already believe? Sartre's detour through the paradox of sincerity allows him
to shed light on the paradox of bad faith by shifting the focus of attention
from the problem of contradictory beliefs to the problematic nature of belief
itself. The "essential problem of bad faith is a problem of belief," he affirms.
Since the deceiver and the believer are one and the same, bad faith "can not
be either a cynical lie or certainty." The only path open to it is to renounce
certainty, resolving "to count itself satisfied when it is barely persuaded, to
force itself in decisions to adhere to uncertain truths." While "bad faith is
conscious of its structure," it is able to persuade itself that it is persuaded
when it is not really persuaded because "it has taken precautions by deciding
. . . that non-persuasion is the structure of all convictions."[40]

At this point the best way to appreciate Sartre's argument is to pause and compare his treatment of bad faith with Davidson's approach to self-deception. Davidsonian self-deception is in good faith. Although one belief is motivated by the desire to get away from another belief, it does not have to skulk about—a barrier protects it from running into the inimical belief. Thanks to the existence of this barrier between contradictory beliefs, self-deception can occur without there being any need to lie to oneself. Indeed, lying to oneself is quite impossible. It is impossible not because one will know the lie isn't true—to believe the lie and to know the truth would in itself entail no more than the existence of contradictory beliefs—but because *one will know one is lying*. What defines a lie is not the liar's disbelief in its content, Davidson observes, but his intentional concealment of his own attitude with respect to this content. A liar must not only "intend to represent himself as believing what he does not," but also "intend to keep this intention . . . hidden from his hearer."[41] It is this metaintention to hide one's intention that poses a special problem in the case of lying to oneself. Can one hide one's own mendacious intent from oneself? Davidson's answer is an unequivocal no.

Sartre's answer to the same question is, just as unequivocally, yes and no. A careful reading of Sartre will reveal that he analyzes the problem of lying to oneself at the same two levels as Davidson. In the ordinary case of lying, Sartre notes, "there is no difficulty in holding that the liar must make the project of the lie in entire clarity and that he must possess a complete comprehension of the lie and of the truth which he is altering." The liar knows the truth and alters it, deceiving another person into believing an untruth. But if the person deceived is oneself, one must simultaneously believe the truth and believe the untruth. Here Sartre is addressing the first level of analysis, the level of contradictory beliefs: How can I believe the lie if I know the truth? Just as the ordinary liar must hide the truth from the other person in order to permit belief in the lie, Sartre assumes that if one is to make oneself believe a lie, one must hide the truth from oneself. I have already quoted Sartre's observation that in lying to oneself, "I must know in my capacity as deceiver the truth which is hidden from me in my capacity as the one deceived." Thus, if bad faith "is indeed a lie to oneself . . . what changes everything is the fact that in bad faith it is from myself that I am hiding the truth."[42]

But the truth is not the only thing I must hide from myself. "To this difficulty is added another which is derived from the total translucency of consciousness." The ordinary liar makes the project of the lie in entire clarity:

"The liar intends to deceive and he does not seek to hide this intention from himself nor to disguise the translucency of consciousness. . . . It is sufficient that an overall opacity hide his intentions from the *Other*." Now, bad faith also entails intention: "consciousness affects itself with bad faith. There must be an original intention and a project of bad faith." But the translucency of consciousness would seem to imply that I cannot hide my own intention to be in bad faith from myself: "That which affects itself with bad faith must be conscious (of) its bad faith." Here Sartre is addressing the second level of analysis, the level of the intention to lie that one must intend to hide from oneself: How can I lie to myself if I know I am lying? Sartre initially acknowledges that I cannot hope to succeed "if I deliberately and cynically attempt to lie to myself."[43]

However, we have seen that for Sartre there is an alternative to such cynicism, and that alternative is bad faith itself. Even if I cannot cynically conceal from myself my intent to persuade myself of something in bad faith, I can always assume an attitude of bad faith with regard to this intent: "at the very moment when I was disposed to put myself in bad faith, I of necessity was in bad faith with respect to this same disposition." In other words, "the project of bad faith must be itself in bad faith." Can one hide one's intent to be in bad faith from oneself after all? Yes and no: "The decision to be in bad faith does not dare to speak its name; it believes itself and does not believe itself in bad faith; it believes itself and does not believe itself in good faith."[44]

A study of the architecture of this last sentence, with its carefully balanced symmetries, will allow us to grasp more clearly the way Sartre has constructed his answer to the question of how one can persuade oneself to believe something in bad faith. There are, we saw, two levels to this construction. The first level is that of the content of the belief: one must deceive oneself into believing something untrue even though one knows the truth. Bad faith at this level entails the coexistence of contradictory beliefs. The second level is that of the intent behind the belief: one must set out to deceive oneself even though one knows one is setting out to deceive oneself. In the sentence in question, Sartre is directly addressing only this second level, but he does so in a way that fully recapitulates his first-level argument. The same analysis applies to both levels since, in order to hide from oneself the true belief, one must also hide from oneself the intent to hide from oneself the true belief. The decision to be in bad faith must itself be in bad faith: it must believe itself to be in good faith even though it believes it is not. Thus, the problem of how to keep hidden from oneself one's intention to deceive likewise comes down to a problem of contradictory beliefs: one must believe one does not intend to deceive oneself even though one knows one does intend to do so.[45]

The foregoing could be summarized, in Sartre's language, by saying that the "decision to be in bad faith" believes itself in bad faith and believes itself in good faith. That indeed is what Sartre says, but he does not leave it at that. The actual sentence that we just saw is considerably more complex. Not only does the "decision" believe itself in bad faith, "it believes itself and does not believe itself in bad faith," and not only does it believe itself in good faith, "it believes itself and does not believe itself in good faith." Sartre's phrasing here is far from arbitrary. It reflects the essential articulation in his argument between the coexistence of contradictory beliefs and the coexistence of belief and disbelief. The possibility of simultaneously believing contradictory propositions rests on the possibility of simultaneously believing and not believing each proposition. Because conscious belief, like conscious sincerity, is impossible, Sartre will argue, it is possible not to believe what one is conscious of believing. Because nonpersuasion is the structure of all convictions, it is possible to believe with conviction what one is conscious of not believing.

For his part, Davidson rejects out of hand the idea that a person may at once believe and not believe: how can one assert such a thing without falling into contradiction oneself? Either people believe or they don't. This objection assumes that the phenomena of consciousness can be described in the same common-sense fashion as an external object, such as a table. But one may question whether it is really common sense not to distinguish consciousness from a table. Sartre establishes such a distinction explicitly. For Sartre, the self-consciousness of consciousness, its presence to itself, paradoxically means that it can never coincide with itself.

Always one step ahead of itself, always just beyond its own grasp, consciousness "must necessarily be what it is not and not be what it is." In this sense, the principle of identity does not apply to consciousness. "Indeed it is impossible to define it as coincidence with itself. Of this table I can say only that it is purely and simply *this* table. But I can not limit myself to saying that my belief is belief; my belief is the consciousness (of) belief."[46] The problem is that "if I know that I believe, the belief appears to me as pure subjective determination," as in the expression "I do not know; I believe so." Hence "to know that one believes is no longer to believe."[47] Here one might retort that Sartre is playing on two meanings of the word "believe." But more than wordplay is involved. Sartre is asserting that a belief in the first sense cannot be known without degenerating into a belief in the second sense. The very nature of belief is transmuted by the reflexivity of consciousness.

By taking the reflexivity of consciousness as the starting point for his argument, Sartre is able to produce a theory of self-deception that is less complicated than Davidson's. More complex, perhaps, and certainly expressed in a more difficult language,[48] but less complicated in the sense of being more parsimonious, of introducing fewer complications. Davidson starts out more straightforwardly in appearance, by decreeing that beliefs are either there or they're not, with no ifs, ands, or buts. The reflexivity of consciousness is thus abstracted out of the overall picture. Yet reflexivity is rightly found to pose a problem when it comes to self-deception. Deception is easy to understand when it takes place between two different people, but not when the deceiver and the deceived are one and the same. As Sartre puts it, "How then can the lie subsist if the duality which conditions it is suppressed?"[49]

Davidson's solution, like Freud's, is to re-create the missing duality by introducing an artificial division within the mind. This solution is consistent with the premise that the mind is a thing like a table, susceptible of being cut into two. Sartre remarks that Freud cuts the psychic whole into two by distinguishing the ego from the id. Davidson is more parsimonious than Freud since he dispenses with the id. But he maintains the minimal complication necessary to produce the desired duality: the idea of a dividing line. The problem is that the only evidence cited for the existence of such a dividing line is the fact of contradictory beliefs. The dividing line cannot explain this fact if its own existence is deduced from the fact to be explained. That would be circular reasoning. As a rule, when a theory begins by suppressing a real circularity intrinsic to its object, that circularity comes back to haunt it in the form of circular reasoning.[50] The suppressed circularity in this case is the one intrinsic to consciousness as a reflexive process.

We don't know that there are dividing lines inside the mind, but we do know that consciousness is reflexive. Indeed, reflexivity is the defining feature of consciousness. In Sartre's terminology, consciousness is present to itself, and he builds his argument on the observation that "*presence to* always implies duality, at least a virtual separation."[51] By showing how the known phenomenon of reflexivity always entails a certain duality, and then relating the duality necessary to understand self-deception to this duality virtually present in all consciousness, Sartre avoids the need to invent an autonomous agent of duality not known to exist. He does not have to hew the mind in two because he has located the duality already latent in the self-reflexive unity of *one and the same* consciousness. It is a paradoxical duality, one that involves phenomenological vicious circles, but the theoretical recognition accorded these real vicious circles spares Sartre from falling into artificial vicious circles in his reasoning.

The phenomenological vicious circles described by Sartre are variants on the type of paradox to which Gregory Bateson, in a paper published the same year as the English translation of *Being and Nothingness*, would give the celebrated name "double bind." A double bind is, in essence, the pragmatic equivalent of the liar's paradox inasmuch as it involves a contradictory self-reference that confuses two different logical levels. The difference is that the liar's paradox can be deemed purely semantic and ruled out of order on the grounds that, by making the accusation of lying refer to itself as its own object, it violates the necessary logical distinction between a statement as a linguistic expression and the object to which a statement refers. The double bind, however, creates an actual pragmatic dilemma for its target by putting the person in the position of obeying a command that can be neither obeyed nor disobeyed, owing to its paradoxical form, and that cannot be ignored either, given the vital nature of the relationship between the individual giving the command and the one receiving it. Thus, where "This statement is false" is a purely semantic paradox, "Disobey this order" is a pragmatic paradox.

Although "Disobey this order" may sound improbably perverse, equivalent injunctions are not so infrequently encountered in families or couples, where one person may reproach the other with not displaying sufficient independence: "You're too submissive; don't always do what I say"; "Love me because you want to and not because I tell you to." Bateson's followers Watzlawick, Beavin, and Jackson observe that injunctions of this type boil down to "Be spontaneous!"[52] If one tries to be spontaneous in response, one is not being spontaneous but merely following orders. But since one is not supposed to follow orders, one is manifesting spontaneity after all—in which case one is doing exactly what one was told. One can neither obey nor disobey because obeying leads to disobeying and disobeying to obeying in a continuous oscillation.

Bateson formulated the hypothesis that pragmatic paradoxes in the communication between parent and child are a factor in the etiology of schizophrenia. In particular, he suggested that a schizophrenic's mother typically sends the child contradictory messages at different levels that keep the child trapped in an oscillation between closeness and distance: "hostile or withdrawing behavior which is aroused whenever the child approaches her" leads to "simulated loving or approaching behavior . . . when the child responds to her hostile and withdrawing behavior, as a way of denying that she is withdrawing." The second message is located at a second level insofar as it constitutes a comment on the first message or sequence of messages: "Yet by its nature it denies the existence of those messages which it is about, *i.e.*, the hostile withdrawal."[53]

The mother's object is to hide from the child and from herself the truth of her own hostility toward the child. This truth threatens to come to the surface whenever the child reacts to her involuntary signs of discomfort in the face of his affectionate approaches. When the child responds to the mother's withdrawal by withdrawing in turn, the mother then scolds the child in a way that reaffirms the mother's loving attitude and puts the onus for the distance between them on the child. For example, the mother of a schizophrenic patient was observed to stiffen when he threw his arm around her shoulders in greeting. When he then withdrew his arm, she asked, "Don't you love me anymore?"[54] The mother acts as an external censor in relation to the child, systematically repressing every manifestation of the child's knowledge of her hostility toward him. But this is not a simple case of the duality between deceiver and deceived. The mother reveals the truth as often as she conceals it; the child is reacting to her own manifestations of hostility. Moreover, the mother's deception undercuts itself to the precise extent that it is successful: if the child responds positively to her feigned affection, she will revert to hostile withdrawal, prompting the child to withdraw once more. And a symmetrical phenomenon is observed on the child's side: any manifestation of belief in the mother's affection undercuts itself by prompting her to withdraw once more.

The self-cancelling character of both the mother's and the child's attempts to conceal the mother's hostility reflects the fact that these symmetrical attempts at deception really involve symmetrical attempts at *self*-deception. The truth of the mother's hostility is accessible to both parties at the level of involuntary communication. Bateson argues that given the importance of the child's relationship to the mother, he will prefer to go along with her reinterpretation of the signals passing between them "rather than recognize his mother's deception. This means that he must deceive himself about his own internal state in order to support mother in her deception." The result is that "the child must systematically distort his perception of metacommunicative signals,"[55] a type of behavior that Bateson relates to the communication pathologies observed in schizophrenic patients. The child must accept at face value his mother's expressions of affection while discounting the metacommunicative signals that contradict them. Given the mother's ill-concealed hostility, her simulated affection may not be very persuasive. For the child to be persuaded, he must adopt a skewed outlook with respect to affective communication in general. To paraphrase Sartre's observation about bad faith, the child must decide that nonpersuasion is the structure of all affections.

The child is deceiving himself insofar as his mother's hostile withdrawal must make him conscious of the truth. At the same time, however, he is aided in the task of self-deception by his mother's periodic gestures of affectionate approach. Similarly, the mother is deceiving herself inasmuch as the child's withdrawal must make her aware of the truth, but she is helped in the task of self-deception by the child's periodic attempts at affectionate approach. The internal duality implied by each person's self-deception is able to subsist thanks to the duality manifested by the other. Just as one sometimes encounters cases of *folie à deux*, we can view this as a case of "self-deception *à deux*." The *pas de deux* of withdrawal and approach between mother and child is an outward manifestation of the "double activity of repulsion and attraction" that Sartre associates with self-deception.

We saw earlier that for Sartre, the "reflexive idea of hiding something from oneself" implies a "double activity" tending at once "to maintain and locate the thing to be concealed" and "to repress and disguise it." Sartre's analysis of self-deception enables us to discover the underlying structure of the maternal double bind described by Bateson: the physical and affective dance of withdrawal and approach derives from the double activity of repulsion and attraction involved in the parties' attempts to conceal from themselves the truth of the mother's hostility. Conversely, Bateson's analysis of the double bind allows us to better grasp the oscillatory logic of bad faith as described by Sartre. Sartre speaks of the "'evanescence' of bad faith," which "vacillates continually between good faith and cynicism."[56] The "double activity" involved in hiding something from oneself turns out to entail a kind of double bind. The difference between Sartre and Bateson is that Bateson identifies double binds in relationships between two people, while Sartre shows that there can be "a double activity in the heart of unity."[57] In Sartre, the internal duality implied by self-deception is not correlated with an external duality, as in Bateson, but with the internal duality implied by self-consciousness. The reflexivity of consciousness means that a paradoxical duality already exists in one's relationship to oneself: "The presence of being to itself implies a detachment on the part of being in relation to itself."[58] And self-deception involves a pragmatic paradox in one's relation to oneself. It is a double bind unfolding within the confines of a single mind.

Sartre does point to a pragmatic paradox in a relationship between two people when he discusses sincerity. As we have seen, the paradox of sincerity brings into play an internal duality similar to that found in bad faith. In fact, Sartre finds in both sincerity and bad faith "the same game of mirrors," a "perpetual passage from the being which is what it is to the being which is not what it is and inversely from the being which is not what it is to the being which is what it is."[59] But sincerity is more likely than bad faith to be the object of an external solicitation. So it is that Sartre comes closest to a paradoxical injunction of the type described by Watzlawick's team when he considers the case of a "champion of sincerity" who insists that the Other confess his nature: "The critic asks the man then to be what he is in order no longer to be what he is"; he demands "that he constitute himself as a thing, precisely in order no longer to treat him as a thing. And this contradiction is constitutive of the demand of sincerity."[60]

The demand "Be sincere!" may sound like the equivalent of "Be spontaneous!" yet this would appear to be only half true. If saying "I am evil" can be a ploy to escape being evil, not being evil does not make one evil again. Confession of sin is, as Sartre notes, a step toward pardon, and pardon does not necessarily return the penitent to being a sinner. Despite Sartre's indications to the contrary, the paradox of sincerity does not display the oscillatory structure characteristic of bad faith. Instead, the paradox of sincerity seems to offer the hope of a one-way ticket out of being what one is. In a sense, this is the principle on which Freudian psychotherapy is founded: if I confess to the analyst what I am, I may find I am able to transcend my previous nature. Similarly, in Alcoholics Anonymous's famous "12-step" approach to overcoming alcoholism—analyzed by Bateson—the "first step demands that the alcoholic agree that he is powerless over alcohol," and this "experience of defeat not only serves to convince the alcoholic that change is necessary; it *is* the first step in that change."[61]

"Be sincere" in these cases is akin to "prescribing the symptom." As we saw previously, prescribing the symptom is a particular form of "Be spontaneous" used by some of Bateson's followers to help a patient assert voluntary control over an undesirable behavioral symptom that ordinarily manifests itself independently of the patient's will—that is to say, spontaneously. Just as the ordinary double bind makes a desirable spontaneity impossible, "prescribing the symptom" operates as a "therapeutic double bind" by rendering an undesirable spontaneity impossible, so that a patient ordered to manifest a pathological behavior may finally succeed in controlling it.[62] To the extent that these pragmatic paradoxes allow me to make a permanent move from *being what I am* to *no longer being what I was*, they are not true double binds. Rather than trapping me in an endless oscillation, they help me out of the trap.

We are now ready to return to the subject of madness with a new question to ask. If confessing what I am is a way of escaping what I am, why shouldn't the same tactic work for a patient suffering from mental illness? Earlier, I raised the possibility that patients may resist recognizing the truth about themselves, and I noted that such resistance could be interpreted as a sign of bad faith. Perhaps if the patient sincerely recognized the truth, a cure could be effected . . . Does the paradox of sincerity offer a way out of madness?

Madness and Sanity: A Paradoxical Divide

The previous discussion could lead one to believe that resistance is the key obstacle to the mental patient's recovery. Whether or not one takes resistance to be in bad faith, one is liable to imagine that a stubborn refusal to accept the truth is the source of all difficulty. If only the patient would recognize he is suffering from delusions, if only the patient would acknowledge he needs help! However, the paradox of self-division proves to be even more stubborn than resistance. For it would be a mistake to think that all psychotics vociferously resist therapy, actively defending their delusions. After observing that patients cannot be treated with dialectical formulas and syllogisms, Esquirol goes on to explain that a patient may "very well know the disorder of his intellectual faculties," follow the therapist's reasoning, and even strive to believe what he is told, and yet still "lack the force of conviction": "I know all that, but my idea is there, and I am not cured."[63]

Esquirol reports the statement of one patient in particular that suggests it is not enough for a psychotic to recognize he needs help: "'If I could believe with you that I am mad, I would soon be cured,' one of them said to me, 'but I cannot acquire this belief.'"[64] Here we have a truly model patient: one who sincerely recognizes he is suffering from delusions, one who acknowledges he needs help. What is the obstacle here to acquiring belief? Not lack of knowledge: the patient implicitly acknowledges the validity of what he is unable to believe. He believes he should believe he is crazy—indeed, he believes quite literally that he is crazy not to: not to believe he is crazy is what keeps him from being cured. Now, to believe he is not yet cured is to believe that he is still crazy. So, on the one hand, he believes he is crazy, and yet, by his own testimony, he does not believe he is crazy: "I cannot acquire this belief." Note that what we have here is not the mere coexistence of contradictory beliefs, but the coexistence of belief and disbelief. Gauchet and Swain speak of a "mysterious and impalpable separation" that can prevent a patient "from receiving completely what he nevertheless succeeds quite well in understanding."[65]

Let us try to get to the bottom of this mystery. What is it that separates the patient from his own belief and keeps his belief and disbelief apart? Is there a wall between them? At this point I would like to propose an image which I think is better than that of a wall. The patient's belief and disbelief are not on opposite sides of a wall—they are on opposite sides of a Möbius strip. They are not separated, for they are inextricably linked, but they are linked in a way that forever keeps them from coming together. In other words, the connection between them is, in the true sense of the word, paradoxical. The best way to understand what I mean by this is to come back to the problem of lying to oneself.

Recall that for Davidson, a liar must not only "intend to represent himself as believing what he does not," but also "intend to keep this intention . . . hidden from his hearer."[66] I tried to show earlier that for Sartre as well as for Davidson, it is this latter intention—the metaintention to keep one's intention hidden—that poses a special problem in the case of lying to oneself. There is nothing paradoxical in the ordinary case of lying to someone else because here the concealment of the intention to deceive is not problematic. As Sartre puts it, "The liar intends to deceive and he does not seek to hide this intention from himself. . . . As for his flaunted intention of telling the truth ('I'd never want to deceive you! This is true! I swear it!')—all this, of course, is the object of an inner negation, but also it is not recognized by the liar as *his* intention."[67] In order to underscore that the concealment of intention is the key to lying—and not, for example, the fact of saying the opposite of what one believes—Davidson observes that "a liar who believes that his hearer is perverse may say the opposite of what he intends his hearer to believe."[68]

What if, instead, it is the liar who is perverse? What if the liar warns the hearer that what he is saying is the opposite of what the hearer should believe: "I want to deceive you! This statement is false! I swear it!" Now we have a case of lying to someone else that is just as paradoxical as lying to oneself—and, I would argue, paradoxical for the same reason. For if it is true that the concealment of the intention to deceive is ordinarily not problematic, the *disclosure* of the intention to deceive *is* problematic, even in the case of lying to someone else. To the extent that this disclosure is self-reflexive, the person on the receiving end is confronted with the liar's paradox. This is just as true if the person on the receiving end is oneself. Lying to oneself is especially susceptible to paradox because one cannot avoid disclosing one's intent to oneself. If I lie to myself, I will know that "I am lying."

Indeed, one may be tempted to conclude that lying to oneself is simply impossible: How can I lie to myself without knowing it? But the question can just as easily be turned around: How can I know it? For if I know I am lying, I cannot conceal from myself my intent to deceive. But if I do not conceal my intent to deceive, I am not lying—and so I cannot know that I am . . . And this lack of knowledge may make it easier for me to lie to myself after all. To be sure, an alternative interpretation would be that by not concealing from myself my intent to deceive, I have quite simply failed in my attempt to lie to myself. Here I would reply by citing Sartre's remark that the essence of bad faith lies in the acceptance of such failure. In fact, it will be recalled, Sartre likewise recognizes the impossibility of deliberately and cynically lying to oneself. To "the extent that I am conscious of my bad faith," he says, then it appears "that I must be in good faith." But in that case "this whole psychic system is annihilated. We must agree in fact that if I deliberately and cynically attempt to lie to myself, I completely fail in this undertaking."[69] However, Sartre later goes on to assert that while "it is very true that bad faith does not succeed in believing in what it wishes to believe," "it is precisely as the acceptance of not believing what it believes that it is bad faith."[70]

In other words, bad faith takes itself for good faith. And, I would add, this possibility is enhanced by the very fact that I am conscious of my bad faith, if it is precisely this fact that allows me to draw the conclusion that "I must be in good faith." Consciousness of bad faith leads to a belief in good faith, the belief in good faith makes bad faith possible, bad faith is accompanied by consciousness of bad faith, and consciousness of bad faith leads to a belief in good faith . . . In short, the belief in bad faith leads to a belief in good faith and the belief in good faith to a belief in bad faith. This psychic system is not annihilated; it oscillates indefinitely in the manner of the liar's paradox.

The oscillatory structure of the liar's paradox or its pragmatic equivalent derives from the presence of a contradictory self-reference confusing logical levels. An ordinary lie merely negates something external to itself, namely, the truth; as Sartre notes, the "negation does not bear on consciousness itself."[71] Lying to oneself is paradoxical not at the level of the consciousness of the truth, but at the level of the consciousness of consciousness. To know I am lying to myself is not to know it: the negation bears on consciousness itself. To set out to lie to oneself therefore means placing oneself in a double bind. Sincere recognition that one is lying will not put an end to the oscillation—it is responsible for it. The paradox of sincerity no longer offers a one-way ticket out of being what one is when what one confesses to being is a liar.

We are now ready to return to the case of the patient who tells the therapist he is not cured of madness because he cannot believe he is mad. In fact, the patient's statement can also be usefully compared to the liar's paradox. If Eubulides says "I am lying," is he lying? His statement is false if it is true and true if it is false. We cannot say whether it is true or false; we can only identify it as a paradoxically twisted metastatement about its own truth or falsity. In the same way, we cannot say whether the patient believes or does not believe he is mad when he says, "I cannot acquire this belief." We can only identify this as the statement of a paradoxically twisted metabelief about his own belief.

The difficulty in interpreting such a statement doubtless represents a tricky problem for the therapist. Gauchet and Swain point out that Esquirol uses the same quotation, or equivalent variants on it, in two completely opposite contexts. The first time that Esquirol quotes the patient's statement "If I could believe I am mad I would soon be cured," it is in order to show how the unexpected care the asylum gives the patient provokes a "salutary shock," a "moral contrast," which may help the patient "glimpse the possibility he is sick; and is not this result the surest token of recovery?" Later in the same book Esquirol provides a new version of the same quotation: "I comprehend very well what you are telling me; I follow quite well your reasoning, if I could understand you and if I could convince myself, I would no longer be crazy, you would have cured me."[72] This time, however, the lesson Esquirol draws is as pessimistic as it was optimistic the first time: the patient's tantalizing lucidity is not enough to accomplish the recovery it seemed to betoken.[73]

The ambivalence of the ways in which Esquirol construes the same quotation is a reflection of the intrinsic ambivalence of the quotation itself. One is tempted to accuse Esquirol of simultaneously entertaining contradictory beliefs about it, as if he were himself ensnared in the paradox. Now, if the paradox is a trap for the therapist who confronts it from the outside, how much more of a trap must it be for the patient who struggles with it from within. The utterance of Esquirol's patient is based on a true insight, the same insight with which we saw Doctor Kora's patient struggle earlier: a sure symptom of madness is that, unlike those around him, the madman does not know he is mad. Thus, when the protagonist of an Isaac Bashevis Singer story discussed by Alfred Mele, "Gimpel the Fool," lets his wife persuade him that her infidelity is only a hallucination on his part, we may take Gimpel's belief that he hallucinated as proof that he is not crazy—he is just a fool. A true madman's disbelief of the fact that he is mad is the wall that separates him from those around him. Our problem is to understand how this disbelief can coexist with knowledge in the absence of an internal wall within the patient. Esquirol's patient is no fool. He knows that if, like Gimpel, he could convince himself he is suffering from delusions, then he would no longer be mad. His knowledge can be summed up as follows: "I am crazy because I don't know I am crazy." But this paradoxical self-knowledge is of no help in moving from being crazy to not being crazy. Like Esquirol, the patient does not know what to believe about what he believes. His belief is not walled off from his disbelief, it is bound to it, but the connection is as twisted as that between opposite sides of a Möbius strip, where each side leads directly to the other. As a result, he is caught up in a perpetual oscillation.

In case the reader is still not persuaded that the paradoxical form of the self-knowledge of madness constitutes the key to the problem, let us try to imagine what it would mean to escape from that paradox. I think we will find that we fall into a catch-22 situation of the purest kind—precisely the one invented by Joseph Heller in his novel of World War II.[74] Everyone is familiar with the dilemma of Heller's antihero, Yossarian. Hoping to avoid flying any more combat missions, Yossarian "decides to go crazy." He consults the medic, Doc Daneeka, who fills him in on the rules. On the one hand, "There's a rule saying I have to ground anyone who's crazy," but, on the other hand, "Anyone who wants to get out of combat duty isn't really crazy." In short, "There was only one catch and that was Catch-22, which specified that a concern for one's own safety in the face of dangers that were real and immediate was the process of a rational mind."[75]

Now, although "catch-22" has become a familiar symbol of the "craziness" of wartime, the "craziness" of bureaucracy, and so on, Yossarian is not really crazy, of course—he just wants to escape the "craziness" of those around him. What may be missed is that the same catch will also apply to someone who really is crazy and is trying to escape his own craziness. For, if instead of saying "I am crazy because I don't know I'm crazy," one cuts through that annoying paradox and goes directly to the required self-knowledge in seemingly unmediated form—"I am crazy"—one finds oneself right smack-dab back in an even purer form of the liar's paradox.[76] As Doc Daneeka tells Yossarian, "you can't let crazy people decide whether you're crazy or not, can you?"[77]

By casting doubt on the judgment of crazy people, Doc Daneeka helps us see why it is so hard to judge oneself crazy. The judgment applies not to any particular deluded belief external to itself, but to the very consciousness doing the judging, and it does so in a way that negates that consciousness.

The negation bears on consciousness itself. If craziness implies a lack of awareness of being crazy, then recognition of being crazy would seem to be necessary in order to stop being crazy. But the sincerest recognition that one is crazy is no better than sincere recognition that one is a liar. Like lying to oneself, recognizing one is crazy means sticking one's head in a double bind. Gregory Bateson's hypothesis is that double binds may contribute to provoking entry into psychosis. In this chapter, I have considered the question from the other end. My hypothesis is that a double bind may contribute to blocking exit from psychosis. If leaving madness necessitated recognizing one is mad, the road from not recognizing one is mad to not being mad could prove impossibly twisted.

That does not mean that madness is an inescapable destiny, but it does underscore the urgency of intervening early. At the same time, it points to a possible therapeutic strategy. If one can't induce the mad to recognize their madness, why not take the opposite tack? That is precisely what Doctor Henri Grivois does. As we saw previously, he tells patients in the midst of a psychotic break that they are in fact experiencing a real event—a singular, astonishing, unsettling event, but one that others have experienced, too. In this way, Doctor Grivois sidesteps the paradox exposed by Doc Daneeka. When one is in the throes of nascent psychosis, one cannot be expected to pronounce oneself crazy, nor is there any need to do so. Later, though, when the storm has passed, perhaps one will be able to look back and say, in a tone of profound relief mixed with disbelief, "You know, I *was* crazy, then."

We are, all of us, mad or not, fated to struggle with the irreducible loopiness of human existence. Often, without even realizing it, we find ourselves caught in double binds or self-fulfilling prophecies of the kind discussed in this book. They are an ever-present trap; they are never a prison. Understanding the tangled loops of violence, myth, and madness is the first step to breaking free of them. The belief that things cannot change is always a myth, no matter how widely shared it may be.

Myth, Girard teaches us, is born of unanimity. Unanimity is the enemy of truth and progress. It is a formidable enemy but a fragile one, for the tiniest minority is capable of breaching it. When an individual stands up against the crowd, when a therapist shows a patient that at least one person treats their experience with respect, unanimity begins to fissure. A crack is opened for the light to get in.

Notes

Chapter 1. Beginning with the Return, or Vengeance in Reverse

1. Claude Lévi-Strauss, *The Elementary Structures of Kinship*, rev. ed., trans. J. H. Bell, J. R. von Sturmer, and R. Needham (Boston: Beacon Press, 1969), 67.

2. Alfred Adler, "La guerre et l'État primitif," in *L'esprit des Lois sauvages: Pierre Clastres ou une nouvelle anthropologie politique*, ed. Miguel Abensour (Paris: Seuil, 1987), 97.

3. See Mark R. Anspach, *À charge de revanche: Figures élémentaires de la réciprocité* (Paris: Seuil, 2002).

4. Raymond Verdier, "Le système vindicatoire: Esquisse théorique," in *La vengeance*, vol. 1, *Vengeance et pouvoir dans quelques sociétés extra-occidentales*, ed. Raymond Verdier (Paris: Cujas, 1980), 11–42.

5. René Girard, *Violence and the Sacred*, trans. Patrick Gregory (Baltimore: Johns Hopkins University Press, 1977), 15.

6. See Lucien Scubla, "Vindicatory System, Sacrificial System: From Opposition to Reconciliation," in *Vengeance*, ed. Mark R. Anspach, special issue, *Stanford French Review* 16, no. 1 (1992): 55–76.

7. Paul Watzlawick, Janet Helmick Beavin, and Don D. Jackson, *Pragmatics of Human Communication: A Study of Interactional Patterns, Pathologies, and Paradoxes* (New York: Norton, 1967), 241.

8. Ibid., 249–50.

9. Verdier, "Le système vindicatoire," 30.

10. René Girard, *Things Hidden since the Foundation of the World*, trans. Stephen Bann and Michael Metteer (Stanford: Stanford University Press, 1987), 79.

11. Watzlawick, Beavin, and Jackson, *Pragmatics of Human Communication*, 248.

12. Ismail Kadare, *Broken April* (New York: New Amsterdam Books, 1990).

13. Ibid., 147.

14. Elizabeth Pond, *Endgame in the Balkans: Regime Change, European Style* (Washington, DC: Brookings Institution, 2006), 193.

15. Dan Bilefsky, "In Albanian Feuds, Isolation Engulfs Families," *New York Times*, July 10, 2008.

16. Miranda Vickers and James Pettifer, *Albania: From Anarchy to a Balkan Identity* (London: Hurst, 1997), 274.

17. Edlira Baka Peco, "Blood-Feud—Internally Displacing Because of Life Security Threat," *Mediterranean Journal of Social Sciences* 5, no. 4 (2014): 509. In a survey conducted by Baka Peco among a random sample of 868 internal migrants living in Bathore, a densely populated shanty town on the outskirts of Tirana, 27.4 percent said they had sought refuge in the capital to escape "conflicts or other incidental problems/blood feud, revenge" (511–13).

18. Bilefsky, "In Albanian Feuds, Isolation Engulfs Families."

19. Colin Freeman, "Albania's Modern-Day Blood Feuds," *The Telegraph*, July 1, 2010.

20. Alfred Adler, "La vengeance du sang chez les Moundang du Tchad," in *La vengeance*, vol. 1, *Vengeance et pouvoir dans quelques sociétés extra-occidentales*, ed. Raymond Verdier (Paris: Cujas, 1980), 75. Adler, "La guerre et l'État primitif," 105.

21. Jean-Pierre Dupuy, "La main invisible et l'indétermination de la totalisation sociale," *Cahiers du CREA* 1 (1982): 55.

22. See Mark R. Anspach, "Tuer ou substituer: L'échange de victimes," *Bulletin du MAUSS* 12 (December 1984): 69–102.

23. Marcel Mauss, *The Gift: The Form and Reason for Exchange in Archaic Societies*, trans. W. D. Halls (New York: W. W. Norton, 1990), 46.

24. Kadare, *Broken April*, 216.

25. At the beginning of the novel, when Gjorg attends the funeral meal for his victim, he cannot stop thinking ahead to the funeral meal that will be held for him. The harsh punishment for vengeance imposed by the Hoxha regime—burying the murderer with the victim—literally collapses their two funerals into one.

26. Jean Baechler, *Les suicides* (Paris: Calmann-Lévy, 1975), 535.

27. Marcel Mauss, "Essai sur le don: Forme et raison de l'échange dans les sociétés archaïques" (first published in *Année Sociologique*, 1923–24), in *Sociologie et anthropologie*, 8th ed. (Paris: Presses Universitaires de France, 1983), 278–79. I have translated the quoted lines myself. The Halls translation omits the original text's reference to avoiding massacres—something that Mauss, writing in the aftermath of World War I, insists the "so-called civilized world" must still learn how to do (*The Gift*, 82–83).

Chapter 2. Violence Deceived

1. See Caroline Gerschlager, introduction to *Expanding the Economic Concept of Exchange: Deception, Self-Deception and Illusions*, ed. Caroline Gerschlager (Boston: Kluwer, 2001), 8.

2. Ibid., 22n16.

3. As suggested by Caroline Gerschlager in her conclusions to *Expanding the Economic Concept of Exchange*, 237.

4. Claude Lévi-Strauss, *The Elementary Forms of Kinship*, rev. ed., trans. J. H. Bell, J. R. von Sturmer, and R. Needham (Boston: Beacon Press, 1967), 67.

5. Marcel Mauss, *The Gift: The Form and Reason for Exchange in Archaic Societies*, trans. W. D. Halls (New York: W. W. Norton, 1990), 81–82.

6. Marcel Mauss, "Essai sur le don: Forme et raison de l'échange dans les sociétés archaïques" (first published in *Année Sociologique*, 1923–24), in *Sociologie et anthropologie*, 8th ed. (Paris: Presses Universitaires de France, 1983), 277.

7. Mauss, *The Gift*, 82.

8. "Rien ne traduit mieux cette instabilité entre la fête et la guerre" (Mauss, "Essai sur le don," 278). I have corrected the published translation of this sentence, which reads: "Nothing better interprets this unstable state between festival and war" (Mauss, *The Gift*, 82). The expression "unstable state" in particular is misleading. Mauss writes "instabilité," not "*état* instable." An in-between *state* would suggest precisely the type of middle term the existence of which he has just excluded.

9. Mauss, *The Gift*, 82.

10. Ibid.

11. Robert H. Lowie, *Primitive Society* (New York: Liveright, 1970), 400, quoted in René Girard, *Violence and the Sacred*, trans. Patrick Gregory (Baltimore: Johns Hopkins University Press, 1977), 16–17.

12. Lowie, *Primitive Society*, 400, quoted in Girard, *Violence and the Sacred*, 25.

13. The Chukchi use the occasion to rid themselves of a relative "whose spitefulness is likely to embroil them with other kins" (Lowie, *Primitive Society*, 400). Executing someone other than the guilty party may appear an aberrant solution to modern eyes, but it is not unique to the Chukchi. Lowie notes that the Australian Dieri "deliberately inflict the death penalty on the criminal's elder brother rather than on the offender himself" (ibid.). One could equally well cite an example from the Solomon Islands. Among the 'Aré'aré, a murder between groups may likewise be settled by having the murderer's group kill one of its own members. In this case, someone who has violated a taboo will be chosen as victim. The final restoration of peace also requires an elaborate exchange of gift payments. See Daniel de Coppet, "The Life-Giving Death," in *Mortality and Immortality: The Anthropology and Archaeology of Death*, ed. S. C. Humphreys and H. King (New York: Academic Press, 1981), 180–81.

14. I have developed this notion in detail elsewhere. See Mark R. Anspach, "Tuer ou substituer: L'échange de victimes," *Bulletin du MAUSS* 12 (December 1984): 69–102.

15. Girard, *Violence and the Sacred*, 25–26.

16. For the purposes of the present discussion, I have simplified somewhat the explanation of how ritual sacrifice works. According to Girard, a double process of substitution is involved. Rather than substituting *directly* for all the members of the community, the sacrificial victim substitutes for an earlier "surrogate victim" who served as a substitute for all the members of the community in some long-ago incident of collective violence. This initial substitution of one for all can be reconstructed from myths of the kind we shall look at in chapter 4. The ritualized violence of sacrifice is modeled on the spontaneous violence of collective scapegoating that such myths

preserve in distorted form. For a more complete summary of Girard's theory of sacrifice, see Mark R. Anspach, "Imitation and Violence: Empirical Evidence and the Mimetic Model," in *Mimesis and Science: Empirical Research on Imitation and the Mimetic Theory of Culture and Religion*, ed. Scott R. Garrels (East Lansing: Michigan State University Press, 2011), 131–36.

17. Note that if the victim and the god can both be equated with the members of the community, it should be no surprise to discover that the victim and the god are one and the same. Girard's theory thus provides a logical explanation for the oft-observed identity of god and victim, which has long represented one of the most baffling problems in the study of religion.

18. Girard, *Violence and the Sacred*, 25.

19. Numerous examples of such rituals will be found in the cross-cultural survey of vengeance published some years after *Violence and the Sacred* by Raymond Verdier, *La Vengeance*, vols. 1–3 (Paris: Cujas, 1980–84); see also Lucien Scubla's analysis in "Vindicatory System, Sacrificial System: From Opposition to Reconciliation," in *Vengeance*, ed. Mark R. Anspach, special issue, *Stanford French Review* 16, no. 1 (1992): 55–76.

20. Pierre Lemonnier, *Guerres et festins: Paix, échanges et compétition dans les Highlands de Nouvelle-Guinée* (Paris: Editions de la Maison des Sciences de l'Homme, 1990), 99.

21. Mauss, "Essai sur le don," 278. I have modified slightly the published translation of this sentence (Mauss, *The Gift*, 82).

22. In reality, the cases of New Guinea and Siberia are not as far apart as one might imagine. Pierre Lemonnier actually describes a shift between two different systems in New Guinea, a more warlike one characterized by identical, flesh-for-flesh reciprocity, and a substitution-based one more oriented toward nonviolent gift exchange. There is a certain parallel to this shift in the societies analyzed by Hamayon, but it is beyond the scope of the present text.

23. Roberte N. Hamayon, "Tricks of the Trade *or* How Siberian Hunters Play the Game of Life-Exchange," in Gerschlager, *Expanding the Economic Concept of Exchange*, 133–37.

24. Ibid., 134.

25. Ibid., 141–42.

26. Ibid., 143.

27. These two observations are probably not unrelated. Unlike the real cases of vengeance between humans discussed earlier, the negative reciprocity between Siberian hunters and animal spirits is a symbolic game played with imaginary partners. A fuller interpretation would have to take into account the extreme form of positive reciprocity imposed by the duty of redistribution, which keeps hunters from consuming their own game (see Hamayon, "Tricks of the Trade," 139). The exaggerated hostility that humans fear from animals might be understood as the counterpart of an exaggerated generosity required from humans in their dealings with fellow humans.

28. Hamayon, "Tricks of the Trade," 137.

29. Ibid., 135.

30. Ibid., 137.

31. Ibid., 145n13.

Chapter 3. Trying to Stop the Trojan War

1. Pierre Crépon, "Le sens des maximes," in *Les Enseignements du Bouddha: Contes et Paraboles* (Paris: Sully, 1999), 105.

2. For example, in the late 1990s, the Kosovo Liberation Army "systematically exposed ethnic Albanian villagers to reprisals by conspicuously turning villages into bases for attack on Serbian police" as part of a "strategy of provocation"; Serbian police retaliation against the KLA was duly stigmatized as "genocide" (Diana Johnstone, *Fools' Crusade* [New York: Monthly Review Press, 2002], 234–35). More recently, Islamic extremists in Lebanon and Gaza have followed a similar strategy, launching missiles at Israel from civilian areas and professing shock at the inevitable counterattacks.

3. Jean-Pierre Dupuy, "Mourning the Future," trans. Reginald McGinnis, *Western Humanities Review* 62, no. 3 (2008): 79–85.

4. Dupuy discusses nuclear war as well as ecological catastrophe in later sections of the book *Petite métaphysique des tsunamis* from which "Mourning the Future" was excerpted (the book as a whole has now been translated by M. B. DeBevoise as *A Short Treatise on the Metaphysics of Tsunamis* [East Lansing: Michigan State University Press, 2015]). Nuclear war is in a category apart because of its absolute nature. In the present chapter we are talking about conventional warfare, which, however great its destructive potential, fails to impress people in the same way as a "doomsday" outcome.

5. Jean Giraudoux, *La guerre de Troie n'aura pas lieu* (Paris: Librairie Générale Française/Le Livre de Poche, 1991), 65. All translations from Giraudoux are mine.

6. René Girard, *Oedipus Unbound: Selected Writings on Rivalry and Desire*, ed. Mark R. Anspach (Stanford: Stanford University Press, 2004), 77.

7. Ibid., 97.

8. Homer, *The Iliad*, trans. Martin Hammond (London: Penguin, 1987), 7.

9. Giraudoux, *La guerre de Troie*, 154.

10. See Jean-Pierre Dupuy, *Pour un catastrophisme éclairé: Quand l'impossible est certain* (Paris: Seuil, 2002), 158.

11. Giraudoux, *La guerre de Troie*, 99.

12. Ibid., 90.

13. See Dupuy, *A Short Treatise*, 7–8.

14. Giraudoux, *La guerre de Troie*, 93–96.

15. The actual German rendering of the title was *Der trojanische Krieg findet nicht statt* (literally, "The Trojan war is not taking place"). See Colette Weil's preface to Giraudoux, *La guerre de Troie*, 6–7.

16. Homer, *The Iliad*, 96.

17. Giraudoux, *La guerre de Troie*, 144.

18. Ibid., 162.

19. Ibid., 82.

20. Girard, *Oedipus Unbound*, 103.

21. Giraudoux, *La guerre de Troie*, 159.

Chapter 4. Return to the Beginning, or the Making of a Metagod

1. Olivier Herrenschmidt, *Les meilleurs dieux sont hindous* (Lausanne: L'Age d'Homme, 1989), 152.

2. William Golding, *Lord of the Flies* (London: Faber and Faber, 1958), 167.

3. Ibid., 97.

4. On the concept of self-transcendence, see Jean-Pierre Dupuy, *Economy and the Future: A Crisis of Faith* (East Lansing: Michigan State University Press, 2014).

5. Luigi Alfieri, "Il fuoco e la bestia: Commento filosofico-politico al *Signore delle Mosche* di Golding," in *Miti Simboli e Politica*, vol. 2, *La contesa tra fratelli*, ed. Giulio M. Chiodi (Turin: Giappichelli, 1993), 228.

6. Charles Malamoud, *Cuire le monde: Rite et pensée dans l'Inde ancienne* (Paris: La Découverte, 1989), 233.

7. Ibid., 237–38.

8. *The Rig Veda*, trans. Wendy Doniger O'Flaherty (Harmondsworth: Penguin, 1981), 31.

9. See A. M. Hocart, *Caste* (London: Methuen, 1950).

10. The ritual in question, performed as part of the preparations for the soma sacrifice, is called the *tānūnaptrá*. See Malamoud, *Cuire le monde*, 227–32; see also Herrenschmidt, *Les meilleurs dieux sont hindous*, 128–29.

11. See Herrenschmidt, *Les meilleurs dieux sont hindous*, 126.

12. Malamoud, *Cuire le monde*, 232.

13. Pascal, *Pensées*, 977 in the Lafuma edition translated by A. J. Krailsheimer, quoted in Andrew McKenna, "Pascal, Order, and Difference," *Religion and Literature* 25, no. 2 (summer 1993): 56.

14. Malamoud, *Cuire le monde*, 232.

15. Cf. Jean-Pierre Dupuy, "The Autonomy of Social Reality: On the Contribution of Systems Theory to the Theory of Society," in *Evolution, Order and Complexity*, ed. Elias L. Khalil and Kenneth E. Boulding (New York: Routledge, 1996), 73.

16. Malamoud, *Cuire le monde*, 232–33.

17. Ibid., 233.

18. A. M. Hocart, *Kingship* (London: Oxford University Press, 1969), 56–57.

19. René Girard, *Violence and the Sacred*, trans. Patrick Gregory (Baltimore: Johns Hopkins University Press, 1977), 8.

20. See Paul Dumouchel and Jean-Pierre Dupuy, eds., *L'auto-organisation: De la physique au politique* (Paris: Seuil, 1983) and, in particular, Paul Dumouchel's contribution, which has been translated into English: "Mimetism and Autonomy," trans. Mary Baker, in Paul Dumouchel, *The Ambivalence of Scarcity and Other Essays* (East Lansing: Michigan State University Press, 2014), 141–54.

21. Golding, *Lord of the Flies*, 103.

22. Malamoud, *Cuire le monde*, 232.

23. Ibid., 234.

24. A. M. Hocart, *Social Origins* (London: Watts, 1954), 77.

25. See Lucien Scubla, "Hocart and the Royal Road to Anthropological Understanding," *Social Anthropology* 10, no. 3 (October 2002): 359–76.

26. "I call the phenomenon a 'trace,'" Hamerton-Kelly explains, because Girard's mimetic model "is not thematic but generative. One does not expect to find its elements unadorned on the surface of the text, rather one sees its generative influence in the contours and seemingly unrelated traces that crop up on the surface" and "are related at a deeper level." See Robert Hamerton-Kelly, "Popular Sovereignty and the Sacred: A Mimetic Reading of Rousseau's Doctrine of the General Will," *Paragrana* 4, no. 2 (1995): 243.

27. Malamoud, *Cuire le monde*, 266.

28. Ibid., 237.

29. To borrow the expression coined by Hyam Maccoby in *The Sacred Executioner* (London: Thames & Hudson, 1982).

30. Herrenschmidt, *Les meilleurs dieux sont hindous*, 153.

31. Ibid., 136, 152.

Chapter 5. Madness in the Making

1. René Girard, *Violence and the Sacred*, trans. Patrick Gregory (Baltimore: Johns Hopkins University Press, 1977), 306.

2. René Girard, "The Founding Murder in the Philosophy of Nietzsche," trans. Mark R. Anspach, in *Violence and Truth: On the Work of René Girard*, ed. Paul Dumouchel (Stanford: Stanford University Press, 1988), 229.

3. Ibid., 231–32.

4. Henri Grivois, "Psychose naissante: La reconstruction du lien," *Cahiers du CREA* 12 (1988): 302.

5. On Girardian theory as a morphogenetic theory, see Jean-Pierre Dupuy, "Mimésis et morphogénèse," in *Ordres et Désordres: Enquête sur un nouveau paradigme* (Paris: Seuil, 1982), 125–85; Jean-Pierre Dupuy, "Totalization and Misrecognition," trans. Mark R. Anspach, in Dumouchel, *Violence and Truth*, 75–100; and Lucien Scubla, "Vers une anthropologie morphogénétique: Violence fondatrice et théorie des singularités," *Le Débat* 77 (1993): 102–20.

6. René Girard, introduction to *"To Double Business Bound": Essays on Literature, Mimesis, and Anthropology* (Baltimore: Johns Hopkins University Press, 1978), xiii.

7. Girard, *Violence and the Sacred*, 301.

8. Girard, introduction to *"To Double Business Bound,"* xiii.

9. Grivois, "Psychose naissante," 297.

10. Ibid., 302.

11. Ibid., 297.

12. Quoted in Dupuy, "Totalization and Misrecognition," 83.

13. Jean-Pierre Dupuy, *La panique* (Paris: Les Empêcheurs de Penser en Rond, 1991), 10.

14. Quoted in Dupuy, "Totalization and Misrecognition," 82.

15. Quoted in ibid., 83.

16. See Dupuy, *La panique*, 58.

17. Ibid., 59.

18. Ibid., 65.

19. Ibid.

20. Dupuy, "Totalization and Misrecognition," 84.

21. Dupuy, *La panique*, 104.

22. The passages quoted here are translated directly from the original French edition: Marcel Gauchet and Gladys Swain, *La pratique de l'esprit humain: L'institution asilaire et la révolution démocratique* (Paris: Gallimard, 1980). Since the initial publication of the present text, an English edition of Gauchet and Swain's work has appeared under the title *Madness and Democracy: The Modern Psychiatric Universe*, trans. Catherine Porter (Princeton, NJ: Princeton University Press, 1999).

23. Gauchet and Swain, *La pratique de l'esprit humain*, 141.

24. Ibid., 145.

25. Jean-Étienne Dominique Esquirol, *Des Maladies mentales* (Paris: Baillière, 1838), quoted in Gauchet and Swain, *La pratique de l'esprit humain*, 144.

26. Henri Grivois, *Naître à la folie* (Paris: Les Empêcheurs de Penser en Rond, 1991), 15–16.

27. Ibid., 87–88.

28. Henri Grivois, "De l'individuel à l'universel: La centralité psychotique," in *Mécanismes mentaux, mécanismes sociaux: De la psychose à la panique*, ed. Henri Grivois and Jean-Pierre Dupuy (Paris: La Découverte, 1995), 39.

29. Gilles Deleuze and Félix Guattari, *L'Anti-Œdipe* (Paris: Minuit, 1972), 101, quoted in René Girard, "Delirium as System," trans. Paisley N. Livingston and Tobin Siebers, in *"To Double Business Bound,"* 85.

30. Grivois, *Naître à la folie*, 25.

31. Gauchet and Swain, *La pratique de l'esprit humain*, 22.

32. Grivois, *Naître à la folie*, 84.

33. Émile Durkheim, *Les formes élémentaires de la vie religieuse* (Paris: Presses Universitaires de France, 1985), 324–25.

34. Ibid., 300–301.

35. Ibid.

36. René Girard, "Strategies of Madness—Nietzsche, Wagner, and Dostoevski," in *"To Double Business Bound,"* 62.

37. Dupuy, "Totalization and Misrecognition," 84.

38. Quoted in Girard, "The Founding Murder," 230.

39. Ibid.

40. See the passage quoted in ibid., 231.

Chapter 6. No Exit? Madness and the Divided Self

1. My retelling of this story is adapted from David K. Reynolds, *Playing Ball on Running Water* (New York: Quill, 1984), 70.

2. Douglas R. Hofstadter, *Gödel, Escher, Bach: An Eternal Golden Braid* (New York: Basic Books, 1979), 690.

3. Donald Davidson, "Deception and Division," in *The Multiple Self*, ed. Jon Elster (Cambridge: Cambridge University Press, 1986), 88–89.

4. Ibid., 91.

5. Alfred R. Mele, "Two Paradoxes of Self-Deception," in *Self-Deception and Paradoxes of Rationality*, ed. Jean-Pierre Dupuy (Stanford: CSLI Publications, 1998), 38.

6. Ibid., 54.

7. Ibid., 57.

8. See Marcel Gauchet and Gladys Swain, *La pratique de l'esprit humain: L'institution asilaire et la révolution démocratique* (Paris: Gallimard, 1980). Since the initial publication of the present text, an English edition of Gauchet and Swain's work has appeared under the title *Madness and Democracy: The Modern Psychiatric Universe*, trans. Catherine Porter (Princeton, NJ: Princeton University Press, 1999).

9. See "Les chaînes qu'on enlève" in Gladys Swain, *Le sujet de la folie: Naissance de la psychiatrie* (Toulouse: Privat, 1977), 119–71. As presented by Swain, the story of Pinel delivering patients from their chains would itself appear to provide a classic example of self-deception: "One believes in it without believing in it, so that objections hardly touch it: it adapts rather well to their proximity, sometimes to the point of coexisting on good terms with them" (119).

10. Swain, *Le sujet de la folie*, 22–23.

11. Ibid., 103.

12. Ibid., 96.

13. Quoted in ibid., 93–94.

14. See Richard Whately, *Historic Doubts Relative to Napoleon Bonaparte*, ed. Ralph S. Pomeroy (Berkeley: Scolar Press, 1985).

15. Gordon Claridge, *Origins of Mental Illness* (New York: Blackwell, 1985), 148.

16. Quoted in Gauchet and Swain, *La pratique de l'esprit humain*, 474–75.

17. Swain, *Le sujet de la folie*, 102.

18. Jean-Paul Sartre, *Being and Nothingness*, trans. Hazel E. Barnes (New York: Washington Square Press, 1966), 89.

19. Ibid., 90–92.

20. Ibid., 93.

21. Ibid., 92–93.

22. Ibid., 90.

23. Sartre goes so far as to claim that the censor in its turn must be "conscious of the drive to

be repressed . . . *in order not to be conscious of it*," so that, in attempting to overcome bad faith, psychoanalysis has merely "established between the unconscious and consciousness an autonomous consciousness in bad faith" (ibid., 94). Larry Beyer has pointed out to me that this assertion of the censor's bad faith is gratuitous. The censor's aim is to keep knowledge of what is repressed from the conscious mind, not from itself. Once we accept the existence of a reified censor, there is no need for the censor to be in bad faith. However, I believe Sartre's argument is sound once shorn of this ill-conceived crowning touch. I take his fundamental criticism to be directed at the very fact of reifying the censor as an autonomous consciousness between consciousness and the unconscious.

24. Sartre, *Being and Nothingness*, 94–95.

25. Simon Boag, "Freudian Dream Theory, Dream Bizarreness, and the Disguise-Censor Controversy," *Neuro-Psychoanalysis* 8, no. 1 (2006): 9–11.

26. Quoted in Boag, "Freudian Dream Theory," 7. Freud is referring specifically to the "censor of dreams" here.

27. Boag, "Freudian Dream Theory," 6.

28. Ibid., 11.

29. Jean-Pierre Dupuy, *Economy and the Future: A Crisis of Faith* (East Lansing: Michigan State University Press, 2014), 28–29.

30. Thus, while Sartre's argument is directed against Freud's theory of the unconscious, it represents a challenge even for a weaker theory of partitioning, such as that defended by Davidson, which does not posit the unconsciousness of any one of the separate territories to which the contradictory beliefs are relegated. "I see no obvious reason to suppose one of the territories must be closed to consciousness, whatever exactly that means," writes Davidson, "but it is clear that the agent cannot survey the whole without erasing the boundaries" ("Deception and Division," 92). This theory would seem to call for a censor to keep the agent from surveying the whole, and if each part of the whole is open to consciousness, the censor's job would appear to be all the harder. In short, to posit the existence of boundaries—even if they are functional rather than physical—does not explain anything unless the functioning of the boundaries can be explained.

31. Sartre, *Being and Nothingness*, 101.

32. Ibid., 105–6.

33. Note that throughout this discussion Sartre is concerned "only with the sincerity which aims at itself in present immanence," and not with the "sincerity which bears on the past" (ibid., 110). I can be sincere about who I was precisely because my past self is already an external object in relation to who I am.

34. Ibid., 106.

35. Ibid., 108–9.

36. Ibid., 109.

37. Ibid., 105.

38. Ibid., 101.

39. Ibid., 111.

40. Ibid., 112–13.

41. Davidson, "Deception and Division," 88.

42. Sartre, *Being and Nothingness*, 88–89.

43. Ibid.

44. Ibid., 112–13.

45. It is not clear what would stop Davidson from making a parallel theoretical move within the terms of his own theory. That is, if contradictory beliefs can coexist separated by a boundary within the mind, why not posit the existence of a like boundary between the knowledge that one intends to lie to oneself and a belief that one does not so intend? There would then be no need to rule out a priori the possibility of lying to oneself.

46. Sartre, *Being and Nothingness*, 120–21.

47. Ibid., 114.

48. Which I have gone out of my way to simplify here as far as possible, even at the risk of oversimplification.

49. Sartre, *Being and Nothingness*, 89.

50. See Mark R. Anspach, "From the Double Bind to Autonomy: Epistemological Challenges in Contemporary French Theory" (PhD diss., Stanford University, 1991).

51. Sartre, *Being and Nothingness*, 124.

52. Paul Watzlawick, Janet Helmick Beavin, and Don D. Jackson, *Pragmatics of Human Communication: A Study of Interactional Patterns, Pathologies, and Paradoxes* (New York: Norton, 1967), 199–200.

53. Gregory Bateson, *Steps to an Ecology of Mind* (New York: Ballantine, 1972), 213.

54. Ibid., 217.

55. Ibid., 214.

56. Sartre, *Being and Nothingness*, 90.

57. Ibid., 94.

58. Ibid., 124.

59. Ibid., 110.

60. Ibid., 108.

61. Bateson, *Steps to an Ecology of Mind*, 312–13.

62. Watzlawick, Beavin, and Jackson, *Pragmatics of Human Communication*, 237.

63. Quoted by Gauchet and Swain in *La pratique de l'esprit humain*, 475.

64. "Si je pouvais croire avec vous que je suis fou, je serais bientôt guéri, me disait l'un d'eux, mais je ne puis acquérir cette croyance." Quoted in Gauchet and Swain, *La pratique de l'esprit humain*, 477.

65. Gauchet and Swain, *La pratique de l'esprit humain*, 475.

66. Davidson, "Deception and Division," 88.

67. Sartre, *Being and Nothingness*, 88.

68. Davidson, "Deception and Division," 88.

69. Sartre, *Being and Nothingness*, 89.

70. Ibid., 115.

71. Ibid., 87.

72. "J'entends très bien ce que vous me dites; je suis bien vos raisonnements, si je pouvais vous comprendre et si je pouvais me convaincre, je ne serais plus fou, vous m'auriez guéri."

73. Quoted in Gauchet and Swain, *La pratique de l'esprit humain*, 477–78.

74. It is said that if James Watt had not invented the steam engine, someone else would have, for the idea was in the air: it was "steam-engine time." In the same way, the period during and after World War II seems to have been "double bind time." *Catch-22*—whose narrative is one long series of pragmatic paradoxes of which the one I discuss in the text is only the most famous example— appeared in 1955. Sartre's discussion of bad faith is part of *Being and Nothingness*, which was published in France during World War II and appeared in English translation in 1956. The same year saw the publication of the paper "Toward a Theory of Schizophrenia" (reprinted in Bateson, *Steps to an Ecology of Mind*, 201–27) in which Gregory Bateson, Don D. Jackson, Jay Haley, and John H. Weakland introduced the term "double bind." Bateson worked in psychological warfare with the Office of Strategic Services during World War II, and he later developed the double bind theory while working with patients in the Veterans Administration Hospital in Palo Alto.

75. Joseph Heller, *Catch-22* (1955; repr., New York: Dell, 1962), 46–47.

76. Cf. Bateson's hypothesis "that the message 'This is play' establishes a paradoxical frame comparable to Epimenides' paradox," to the extent that the message can be rephrased "All statements within this frame are untrue" and that this statement "is itself to be taken as a premise in evaluating its own truth or untruth." Bateson anticipates an objection to this hypothesis: "It could be urged that even if the first statement is false, there remains a logical possibility that some of the other statements in the frame are untrue." Bateson's response is to note that it is "a characteristic of unconscious or 'primary-process' thinking that the thinker is unable to discriminate between 'some' and 'all,' and unable to discriminate between 'not all' and 'none.' It seems that the achievement of these discriminations is performed by higher or more conscious mental processes which serve in the nonpsychotic individual to correct the black-and-white thinking of the lower levels" (*Steps to an Ecology of Mind*, 184–85).

I would argue that "I am crazy" should not be rephrased "All statements within this frame are untrue." The delusions of the mad can easily be limited in number rather than all-encompassing. What is at issue is less particular deluded beliefs than craziness as an overall outlook. "I am crazy" is not a statement about what is contained in the frame, but a statement about the frame itself. It could therefore be rephrased "This statement is untrue."

77. Heller, *Catch-22*, 46.

Bibliography

Adler, Alfred. "La guerre et l'État primitif." In *L'esprit des Lois sauvages: Pierre Clastres ou une nouvelle anthropologie politique*, edited by Miguel Abensour, 95–114. Paris: Seuil, 1987.

———. "La vengeance du sang chez les Moundang du Tchad." In *La vengeance*, vol. 1, *Vengeance et pouvoir dans quelques sociétés extra-occidentales*, edited by Raymond Verdier, 75–89. Paris: Cujas, 1980.

Alfieri, Luigi. "Il fuoco e la bestia: Commento filosofico-politico al *Signore delle Mosche* di Golding." In *Miti Simboli e Politica*, vol. 2, *La contesa tra fratelli*, edited by Giulio M. Chiodi, 227–63. Turin: Giappichelli, 1993.

Anspach, Mark R. *À charge de revanche: Figures élémentaires de la réciprocité*. Paris: Seuil, 2002.

———. "From the Double Bind to Autonomy: Epistemological Challenges in Contemporary French Theory." PhD diss., Stanford University, 1991.

———. "Imitation and Violence: Empirical Evidence and the Mimetic Model." In *Mimesis and Science: Empirical Research on Imitation and the Mimetic Theory of Culture and Religion,* edited by Scott R. Garrels, 129–54. East Lansing: Michigan State University Press, 2011.

———. "Tuer ou substituer: L'échange de victimes." *Bulletin du MAUSS* 12 (December 1984): 69–102.

Baechler, Jean. *Les suicides*. Paris: Calmann-Lévy, 1975.

Baka Peco, Edlira. "Blood-Feud—Internally Displacing Because of Life Security Threat." *Mediterranean Journal of Social Sciences* 5, no. 4 (2014): 509–15.

Bateson, Gregory. *Steps to an Ecology of Mind*. New York: Ballantine, 1972.

Bilefsky, Dan. "In Albanian Feuds, Isolation Engulfs Families." *New York Times*, July 10, 2008.

Boag, Simon. "Freudian Dream Theory, Dream Bizarreness, and the Disguise-Censor Controversy." *Neuro-Psychoanalysis* 8, no. 1 (2006): 5–16.

Claridge, Gordon. *Origins of Mental Illness.* New York: Blackwell, 1985.

Coppet, Daniel de. "The Life-Giving Death." In *Mortality and Immortality: The Anthropology and Archaeology of Death*, edited by S. C. Humphreys and H. King, 175–204. New York: Academic Press, 1981.

Crépon, Pierre. *Les Enseignements du Bouddha: Contes et Paraboles.* Paris: Sully, 1999.

Davidson, Donald. "Deception and Division." In *The Multiple Self*, edited by Jon Elster, 79–92. Cambridge: Cambridge University Press, 1986.

Dumouchel, Paul. "Mimetism and Autonomy." Translated by Mary Baker. In *The Ambivalence of Scarcity and Other Essays*, 141–54. East Lansing: Michigan State University Press, 2014.

Dumouchel, Paul, and Jean-Pierre Dupuy, eds. *L'auto-organisation: De la physique au politique.* Paris: Seuil, 1983.

Dupuy, Jean-Pierre. "The Autonomy of Social Reality: On the Contribution of Systems Theory to the Theory of Society." In *Evolution, Order and Complexity*, edited by Elias L. Khalil and Kenneth E. Boulding, 61–88. New York: Routledge, 1996.

———. *Economy and the Future: A Crisis of Faith.* East Lansing: Michigan State University Press, 2014.

———. "La main invisible et l'indétermination de la totalisation sociale." *Cahiers du CREA* 1 (1982): 35–60.

———. "Mimésis et morphogénèse." In *Ordres et Désordres: Enquête sur un nouveau paradigme*, 125–85. Paris: Seuil, 1982.

———. "Mourning the Future." Translated by Reginald McGinnis. *Western Humanities Review* 62, no. 3 (2008): 79–85.

———. *La panique.* Paris: Les Empêcheurs de Penser en Rond, 1991.

———. *Pour un catastrophisme éclairé: Quand l'impossible est certain.* Paris: Seuil, 2002.

———. *A Short Treatise on the Metaphysics of Tsunamis.* Translated by M. B. DeBevoise. East Lansing: Michigan State University Press, 2015.

———. "Totalization and Misrecognition." Translated by Mark R. Anspach. In *Violence and Truth: On the Work of René Girard*, edited by Paul Dumouchel, 75–100. Stanford: Stanford University Press, 1988.

Durkheim, Émile. *Les formes élémentaires de la vie religieuse.* Paris: Presses Universitaires de France, 1985.

Freeman, Colin. "Albania's Modern-Day Blood Feuds." *The Telegraph*, July 1, 2010.

Gauchet, Marcel, and Gladys Swain. *Madness and Democracy: The Modern Psychiatric Universe.* Translated by Catherine Porter. Princeton, NJ: Princeton University Press, 1999.

———. *La pratique de l'esprit humain: L'institution asilaire et la révolution démocratique.* Paris: Gallimard, 1980.

Gerschlager, Caroline, ed. *Expanding the Economic Concept of Exchange: Deception, Self-Deception and Illusions.* Boston: Kluwer, 2001.

Girard, René. "The Founding Murder in the Philosophy of Nietzsche." Translated by Mark R. Anspach. In *Violence and Truth: On the Work of René Girard*, edited by Paul Dumouchel, 227–46. Stanford: Stanford University Press, 1988.

———. *Oedipus Unbound: Selected Writings on Rivalry and Desire*. Edited by Mark R. Anspach. Stanford: Stanford University Press, 2004.

———. *Things Hidden since the Foundation of the World*. Translated by Stephen Bann and Michael Metteer. Stanford: Stanford University Press, 1987.

———. *"To Double Business Bound": Essays on Literature, Mimesis, and Anthropology*. Baltimore: Johns Hopkins University Press, 1978.

———. *Violence and the Sacred*. Translated by Patrick Gregory. Baltimore: Johns Hopkins University Press, 1977.

Giraudoux, Jean. *La guerre de Troie n'aura pas lieu*. Paris: Librairie Générale Française/Le Livre de Poche, 1991.

Golding, William. *Lord of the Flies*. London: Faber and Faber, 1958.

Grivois, Henri. "De l'individuel à l'universel: La centralité psychotique." In *Mécanismes mentaux, mécanismes sociaux: De la psychose à la panique*, edited by Henri Grivois and Jean-Pierre Dupuy, 23–65. Paris: La Découverte, 1995.

———. *Naître à la folie*. Paris: Les Empêcheurs de Penser en Rond, 1991.

———. "Psychose naissante: La reconstruction du lien." *Cahiers du CREA* 12 (1988): 291–307.

Hamayon, Roberte N. *Jouer: Étude anthropologique à partir d'exemples sibériens*. Paris: La Découverte, 2012.

———. "Tricks of the Trade *or* How Siberian Hunters Play the Game of Life-Exchange." In *Expanding the Economic Concept of Exchange: Deception, Self-Deception and Illusions*, edited by Caroline Gerschlager, 133–47. Boston: Kluwer, 2001.

———. *Why We Play: An Anthropological Study*. Translated by Damien Simon. Chicago: Hau Books, 2016.

Hamerton-Kelly, Robert. "Popular Sovereignty and the Sacred: A Mimetic Reading of Rousseau's Doctrine of the General Will." *Paragrana* 4, no. 2 (1995): 215–44.

Heller, Joseph. *Catch-22*. New York: Dell, 1962.

Herrenschmidt, Olivier. *Les meilleurs dieux sont hindous*. Lausanne: L'Age d'Homme, 1989.

Hocart, A. M. *Caste*. London: Methuen, 1950.

———. *Kingship*. London: Oxford University Press, 1969.

———. *Social Origins*. London: Watts, 1954.

Hofstadter, Douglas R. *Gödel, Escher, Bach: An Eternal Golden Braid*. New York: Basic Books, 1979.

———. *I Am a Strange Loop*. New York: Basic Books, 2007.

Homer. *The Iliad*. Translated by Martin Hammond. London: Penguin, 1987.

Johnstone, Diana. *Fools' Crusade*. New York: Monthly Review Press, 2002.

Kadare, Ismail. *Broken April*. New York: New Amsterdam Books, 1990.

Lemonnier, Pierre. *Guerres et festins: Paix, échanges et compétition dans les Highlands de Nouvelle-Guinée.* Paris: Editions de la Maison des Sciences de l'Homme, 1990.

Lévi-Strauss, Claude. *The Elementary Structures of Kinship.* Rev. ed. Translated by J. H. Bell, J. R. von Sturmer, and R. Needham. Boston: Beacon Press, 1969.

Lowie, Robert H. *Primitive Society.* New York: Liveright, 1970.

Maccoby, Hyam. *The Sacred Executioner.* London: Thames & Hudson, 1982.

Malamoud, Charles. *Cuire le monde: Rite et pensée dans l'Inde ancienne.* Paris: La Découverte, 1989.

Mauss, Marcel. "Essai sur le don: Forme et raison de l'échange dans les sociétés archaïques." In *Sociologie et anthropologie*, 8th ed., 143–279. Paris: Presses Universitaires de France, 1983.

———. *The Gift: The Form and Reason for Exchange in Archaic Societies.* Translated by W. D. Halls. New York: W. W. Norton, 1990.

McKenna, Andrew. "Pascal, Order, and Difference." *Religion and Literature* 25, no. 2 (summer 1993): 55–75.

Mele, Alfred R. "Two Paradoxes of Self-Deception." In *Self-Deception and Paradoxes of Rationality*, edited by Jean-Pierre Dupuy, 37–58. Stanford: CSLI Publications, 1998.

Pond, Elizabeth. *Endgame in the Balkans: Regime Change, European Style.* Washington, DC: Brookings Institution, 2006.

Reynolds, David K. *Playing Ball on Running Water.* New York: Quill, 1984.

The Rig Veda. Translated by Wendy Doniger O'Flaherty. Harmondsworth: Penguin, 1981.

Sartre, Jean-Paul. *Being and Nothingness.* Translated by Hazel E. Barnes. New York: Washington Square Press, 1966.

Scubla, Lucien. "Hocart and the Royal Road to Anthropological Understanding." *Social Anthropology* 10, no. 3 (October 2002): 359–76.

———. "Vers une anthropologie morphogénétique: Violence fondatrice et théorie des singularités." *Le Débat* 77 (1993): 102–20.

———. "Vindicatory System, Sacrificial System: From Opposition to Reconciliation." In *Vengeance*, edited by Mark R. Anspach, special issue, *Stanford French Review* 16, no. 1 (1992): 55–76.

Shergill, Sukhwinder S., Paul M. Bays, Chris D. Frith, and Daniel M. Wolpert. "Two Eyes for an Eye: The Neuroscience of Force Escalation." *Science* 301 (July 11, 2003): 187.

Swain, Gladys. *Le sujet de la folie: Naissance de la psychiatrie.* Toulouse: Privat, 1977.

Verdier, Raymond. "Le système vindicatoire: Esquisse théorique." In *La vengeance*, vol. 1, *Vengeance et pouvoir dans quelques sociétés extra-occidentales*, edited by Raymond Verdier, 11–42. Paris: Cujas, 1980.

Vickers, Miranda, and James Pettifer. *Albania: From Anarchy to a Balkan Identity.* London: Hurst, 1997.

Watzlawick, Paul, Janet Helmick Beavin, and Don D. Jackson. *Pragmatics of Human Communication: A Study of Interactional Patterns, Pathologies, and Paradoxes.* New York: Norton, 1967.

Whately, Richard. *Historic Doubts Relative to Napoleon Bonaparte.* Edited by Ralph S. Pomeroy. Berkeley: Scolar Press, 1985.

Index

A

Achilles, 31, 35
Adler, Alfred, 4, 9
Agamemnon, 31
Albania: blood feuds in, 7–9, 49, 102n17; fall of communism in, 8
Alcoholics Anonymous, 93
Alfieri, Luigi, 44
Andromache, 29, 33, 38
animal sacrifice, 22–24, 44
'Aré'aré people, 103n13
armor: of Achilles, 31; of Diomedes and Glaukos, 34–37
Asuras, 45, 46
auction house, 82

B

bad faith, 79–87, 91–93, 96, 110n23
Baka Peco, Edlira, 102n17
Bangaramma, 43
Bateson, Gregory, 6, 9, 79, 89, 90–92, 93, 99, 112n74, 112n76
Bayreuth, 68
Being and Nothingness, 89, 112n74
belief: in all-powerful god, 39; coexistence with disbelief, 87, 94, 109n9; consciousness of, 87–88; in contradictory or incompatible propositions, 74–88, 94, 97, 111n45; inability to acquire, 94, 97; problematic nature of, 84; religious, 78
Bellerophontes, 34–35
benevolence: of divinity, 49, 54; of hunters, merchants, and stock-breeders, 24
Beyer, Larry, 110n23
Boag, Simon, 81–82
Broken April, 7–8, 10–11, 31
burying alive, 8, 102n25

C

Cassandra, 28, 29, 30, 32, 33, 38
caste system, 45
catastrophes, 28, 32, 105n4
catch-22, 51, 74, 98
Catch-22, 98, 112n74
censor: external, 90; internal, 81–83, 110n23
Chukchi people, 18–19, 21, 26, 103n13
circular reasoning, 88
Claridge, Gordon, 78
collective effervescence, 44, 67
"concernedness," 65, 66, 68
consciousness, 81, 83, 84, 110n23; disturbed by intense social life, 67; reflexivity of, 87–89,

96; translucency of, 80, 85–86
Coppet, Daniel de, 103n13
crowd, 60–63, 66–71

D

dance, 44
Daribi people, 22
Davidson, Donald, 74, 85, 87, 88, 95, 110n30,
    111n45
Deleuze, Gilles, 66
desire: anticipation of, in gift exchange, 37;
    anticipation of, in market exchange, 24; to
    kill, 39
destiny, 28, 32, 38–39, 54
Dieri people, 103n13
Diomedes, 34–35, 36–37, 38
divination, 25–26
divinity. *See* god
Dobu, 15
Doc Daneeka (*Catch-22*), 98, 99
double binds, 6, 74, 89–92, 93, 96, 99, 112n74
Dupuy, Jean-Pierre, 9, 28, 32, 36, 47, 61–63, 64,
    68, 82
Durkheim, Émile, 44, 49, 66, 67–68

E

Ecce Homo, 68
Echo (Greek myth), 62
ego, 80, 88
Elementary Structures of Kinship, The, 4
Esquirol, Étienne, 64, 70, 78, 94, 97, 98
equilibrium, emergent, 82
exchange: with animals, 23–26; of armor, 34–37;
    and deception, 13–14; distinct from
    reciprocity, 4–5, 10; peaceful, 4, 5, 13–14,
    16–17, 21, 36. *See also* gift exchange
expulsion, 70–71

F

fate, 28, 32, 38–39, 54
feuds. *See* vengeance
fixed points, 47–48, 54, 82
Freud, Sigmund, 61–63, 65, 68, 77, 80–82, 88,
    110n30
funeral rites, 52, 102n25

G

Gauchet, Marcel, 64, 66, 70, 76, 94, 97
generosity, 14–15, 21, 104n27
Gerschlager, Caroline, 13

Gift, The, 10, 14–16
gift exchange, 9–10, 11, 14–22, 35, 36–37, 103n13,
    104n22; with animals, 25
"Gimpel the Fool," 97
Girard, René, x, 4–5, 7, 10, 19–21, 30–31, 38, 49,
    50, 52, 57–60, 66, 68, 69, 99, 103–4nn16–17,
    107n26
Giraudoux, Jean, 29, 30–34, 37–39, 54
Gjorg (*Broken April*), 10–11, 31, 102n25
Glaukos, 34–35, 36–37, 38
god: belief in, 39; death of, 58; identity with
    collectivity, 44, 66; identity with victim,
    104n17; substitute for community, 19–20
Gödel, Escher, Bach, 74
Golding, William, 44, 46, 50
Grivois, Henri, x, 58, 59–60, 61, 64–66, 68, 69,
    70, 99
Group Psychology and the Analysis of the Ego, 61
Guattari, Félix, 66
guerre de Troie n'aura pas lieu, La, 29, 30–34,
    37–39, 54
Guerres et festins, 22
guest-friendship, 34, 36

H

Hamayon, Roberte, 22–26, 104n22
Hamerton-Kelly, Robert, 52, 107n26
hate, 28, 39
Hector, 29, 30–33, 35, 37–39
Hegel, Georg, 77
Helen, 29, 30, 31, 32–33, 37
Heller, Joseph, 98
Hercules, 29
Herrenschmidt, Olivier, 43, 54–55
Hesione, 29
Historic Doubts Relative to Napoleon Bonaparte,
    78
Hocart, A. M., 49, 52
Hofstadter, Douglas, x, 74
Homer, 34
hospitality, 14, 28, 30, 35, 36
Hoxha, Enver, 8, 102n25
human sacrifice, 43–44, 54–55
hunting, 22–26, 38, 44

I

id, 80, 88
Ifugao people, 18
Iliad, 31, 34–37, 38, 45
incest, 52

Indra, 46–48, 50, 53–54, 63, 82
Introductory Lectures on Psycho-Analysis, 81

K

Kadare, Ismail, 7–8, 10–11, 31
kings, 46–47, 50, 52
Kiriwina, 15
Kora, Takehisa, 73, 97

L

leader: of crowd, 61–63, 65, 68–69; without a
    crowd, 62, 67; Indra chosen as, 46; and war,
    28–29
Lemonnier, Pierre, 22, 104n22
Lévi-Strauss, Claude, 4, 14, 15, 16, 21
liar's paradox, 89, 95, 96, 98, 112n76
Lord of the Flies, 44, 46, 50
love, 61–62, 69
Lowie, Robert, 18
lying to oneself, 85–86, 94–96, 111n45
lynching, 52. *See also* violence: collective

M

Madman, Nietzsche's, 58, 69–70, 71
madness, 58–61, 63–71, 73–79, 93–94, 96–99.
    See also mental illness; nascent psychosis;
    schizophrenia
Malamoud, Charles, 9, 44–46, 50, 51, 52, 53–54
Malinowski, Bronislaw, 15
market economy, 24, 82
Mauss, Marcel, 10, 11, 14–16, 18, 21, 22, 34, 37,
    102n27
megalomania, 64
Mele, Alfred, 74, 97
memory of future, 32, 36
Menelaus, 29, 30, 37
mental illness: etiology of, 66, 75; moral
    treatment of, 76, 78
metagod, 46, 48, 50, 52, 54, 82
mimetic theory: as a generative or morphogenetic
    theory, 58, 107n26; sacrificial substitution
    in, 103–4n16; and voluntary human action,
    55
miracles, 43–44, 54–55
Möbius strip, 94, 98
multiple personalities, 75
myth: of Cassandra, 28; circularity in, 50–51;
    of dismembered primordial man, 45;
    of Echo and Narcissus, 62; Girard on,
    59, 99, 104n16; of Indra, 46–52, 63; as

interpretation of real event, 59; of Prajapati
    and Rudra, 52–55; of Trojan war, 29–30;
    and unanimity, 99

N

narcissism, 61–65, 69
nascent psychosis, 59–60, 64–71, 99
New Guinea, 22, 104n22
Nietzsche, Friedrich, 58, 62, 68
nuclear war, 105n4

O

objects: of contention, 4–5; destruction of, 18; of
    exchange, 3, 4, 10, 11, 18; as mediator, 4
Oineus, 34–35
Origins of Mental Illness, 78
Outline of Psychoanalysis, 77

P

pain, telescoping of, 7
Palo Alto school, 6, 7
panic, 61–63
pardon, 92
Paris (Trojan prince), 29, 30, 32
partitioning, mental, 74–75, 76, 77, 79, 83, 110n30
Pascal, Blaise, 47
Patroclus, 31, 35
peace: instability of, 15–17, 37; making, 21–22, 51,
    103n13; seeing, 33, 34, 36; will to, 16
Pinel, Philippe, 76, 77, 78, 109n9
Pond, Elizabeth, 8
potlatch, 11, 18
Prajapati, 52–54, 55
pratique de l'esprit humain, La, 76
prescribing the symptom, 6–7, 93
Priam, 29
Primitive Society, 18
prophecies, 27–28, 32, 33
provocateurs, 28
pseudo-narcissism, 62
psychoanalysis, 80–82
psychosis, nascent, 59–60, 64–71, 99
"punctuation" (of conflict), 9, 29–30, 51

Q

quasi-subject, 32

R

reciprocity, ix–xi; distinct from exchange, 4–5,
    10; negative and positive, 5, 9–11, 14, 17–26,

35–37, 104n27; reversal in orientation of, 5, 9–11, 19, 21–24, 26, 36–37; of undifferentiated antagonists, 31. *See also* gift exchange; vengeance

redistribution, 104n27

reductionism, 57–58

refuge towers, 7–8

repression, 80–82

resistance, 79, 80, 93

revenge. *See* vengeance

Rig Veda, 45

Rousseau, Jean-Jacques, 52

Rudra, 52–54, 55

S

sacred executioner, 54

sacrifice, 19–24, 43–44, 45, 46, 52, 53; animal, 22–24, 44; food sharing in, 21; of gift object, 10, 11; Girard on, 19–21, 52, 59, 103–4n16; human, 43–44, 54–55; of self, 10, 11, 25; of soma, 106n10

sacrificial crisis, 60, 66

Sartre, Jean-Paul, 79–92, 95, 96, 110n23, 110n30, 110n33, 112n74

scapegoating, 52, 55, 60, 104n16

schizophrenia, 66, 68, 78, 79, 90–91

Scubla, Lucien, 5

self-deception, 20, 74–76, 79–85, 88, 89, 91–92, 109n9

self-division, 75, 76, 79, 94

self-exteriorization, 63–64, 68–69

self-fulfilling prophecy, 28, 33, 34, 36, 99

self-interest, 24

self-organization, 50

self-refuting prophecy, 28

self-sacrifice, 10, 11, 25

self-transcendence, 44, 46, 48, 49, 54, 63, 82

seppuku, 11

shamans, 25–26

Siberian hunters, 22–26, 104n22, 104n27

sincerity, 83–84, 92–93, 96, 110n33

Singer, Isaac Bashevis, 97

Smith, Adam, 24

Smith, Robertson, 21

social bond, 45, 52, 60–61, 71

social contract, 45, 49–50, 52

Solomon Islanders, 103n13

soma sacrifice, 106n10

spear, laying down of, 22, 34

Starobinski, Jean, 65

stock-breeding, 22–24

substitution: of animal for human victim, 22–24; of exchange object for giver, 10, 18; of gifts and trade for war, 16, 22; of one murder victim for another, 38; of sacrificial god for community, 19–20; of sacrificial victim for community, 19; of sacrificial victim for surrogate victim, 103–4n16; of shaman for community, 25; of some individuals for all, 26; of surrogate victim for community, 104n16

suicide, 11, 30, 31, 60

sun god, 47–48, 53, 63

superman, Nietzsche's, 62, 68–69

surrogate victim, 38, 49, 57–58, 69, 71, 104n16

Swain, Gladys, 64, 66, 70, 76–77, 79, 94, 97, 109n9

symmetry, 30

T

tānūnaptrá ritual, 106n10

tauschen, similarity with *täuschen*, 13

telescoping: of pain, 7; of vengeance, 7–8

temporal orientation, change in, 9–11, 18–20, 23, 36

terrorists, 28

Tiger at the Gates. See Guerre de Troie n'aura pas lieu, La

tragedy, Greek, 30

transgressors, punishment of, 50–53, 103n13

Trobriand Islanders, 15

Trojan war, 29–39

Trojan War Will Not Take Place, The. See Guerre de Troie n'aura pas lieu, La

trophies, 31, 35, 36

truces, 7

Tungus people, 26

turbulence, 63, 64

Tylor, Edward B., 20

U

Ulysses, 31–32, 37, 39

unanimity, 44, 46, 54, 55, 59, 69, 99; minus one, x, 60, 65, 70–71

unconscious, the, 77, 80–81, 110n23, 110n30, 112n76

undifferentiation, 30–31

V

vendettas. *See* vengeance

vengeance, 3, 5–11, 17–19, 21, 27, 29–31, 35–38,
    102n17, 104n19; of animals, 23–26, 104n27;
    in Japan, 11; opposite of, ix–x; prohibition
    on, 5, 8; reversal of, ix, 11
Verdier, Raymond, 5, 7
vindicatory system, 5–6, 7, 8
violence: collective, 38, 44, 49, 52, 58, 60, 69,
    104n16; deception of, 11, 13–14, 18–20,
    22; displacement of, 10, 18–19, 21, 38;
    nonreciprocal, x; provocation of, 27–28,
    105n2; reciprocal, ix, 7, 19; of sacrifice, 53
Violence and the Sacred, 5, 19

W
Wagner, Richard, 68

Walras, Léon, 82
war, ix, 4, 11, 14–16, 21–22, 28–29, 105n2; nuclear,
    105n4; Trojan, 29–39
Watzlawick, Paul, 6, 89
Whately, Richard, 78
World War I, 102n27
World War II, 98, 112n74

Y
Yossarian (*Catch-22*), 98

Z
Zog, King, 8